Reality Television and the Art of Trivialising Work Health, Safety and Wellbeing

Trajce Cvetkovski

Reality Television and the Art of Trivialising Work Health, Safety and Wellbeing

palgrave
macmillan

Trajce Cvetkovski
Peter Faber Business School
Australian Catholic University
Brisbane, QLD, Australia

ISBN 978-3-031-64097-1   ISBN 978-3-031-64098-8 (eBook)
https://doi.org/10.1007/978-3-031-64098-8

© The Editor(s) (if applicable) and The Author(s), under exclusive license to Springer Nature Switzerland AG 2024

This work is subject to copyright. All rights are solely and exclusively licensed by the Publisher, whether the whole or part of the material is concerned, specifically the rights of translation, reprinting, reuse of illustrations, recitation, broadcasting, reproduction on microfilms or in any other physical way, and transmission or information storage and retrieval, electronic adaptation, computer software, or by similar or dissimilar methodology now known or hereafter developed.
The use of general descriptive names, registered names, trademarks, service marks, etc. in this publication does not imply, even in the absence of a specific statement, that such names are exempt from the relevant protective laws and regulations and therefore free for general use.
The publisher, the authors and the editors are safe to assume that the advice and information in this book are believed to be true and accurate at the date of publication. Neither the publisher nor the authors or the editors give a warranty, expressed or implied, with respect to the material contained herein or for any errors or omissions that may have been made. The publisher remains neutral with regard to jurisdictional claims in published maps and institutional affiliations.

Cover credit: © Harvey Loake

This Palgrave Macmillan imprint is published by the registered company Springer Nature Switzerland AG
The registered company address is: Gewerbestrasse 11, 6330 Cham, Switzerland

If disposing of this product, please recycle the paper.

Acknowledgements

I am very grateful to Laura Papadimos for assistance in data conversion from the coding sheets, time stamping and accurate table formatting. Any errors of omission or commission are the responsibility of the researcher.

SYNOPSIS

How popular culture shapes attitudes towards workplace health, safety and wellbeing (WHSW) has received little attention in the literature. This research remedies this deficiency by examining whether some aspects of workers' HSW are trivialised (if at all) in the Australian construction and renovation reality television show, The Block. Adopting an observational approach, the entire Season 16 (2020) (n=50 episodes) was critically reviewed to assess the level of trivialisation of both identifiable hazards and low order controls. The observations focussed on workplace activities generally perceived or deemed as not high risk or not likely dangerous in the traditional WHSW sense. Nevertheless, such activities are regulated. A cultural theory of risk perception was applied to what appeared to be instances of trivialisation dissonance in relation to attitudes about certain behaviours and practices at the workplace. The following propositions were tested: (1) onsite skylarking, inattention and lax PPE usage were tolerated or downplayed in certain instances; (2) safety signage compliance was inconsistent throughout the season; (3) site untidiness and occasional hygiene issues were observed; (4) onsite consumption and promotion of alcohol appeared to be normalised; (5) antiquated gendered language or stereotyping was used; and (6) potential exposure to various psychosocial hazards was accepted or inadequately addressed on occasion. The goal of the research was to consider the observational data in a system of work setting. Three key themes emerged as a result of critically assessing the show. First, there was a perception that administrative and lower-wrung interventions were inconsistently applied and monitored during the season. Secondly, a culture of alcohol at work was normalised. Thirdly, psychosocial hazard awareness was either inadequate or undervalued. The findings support a cultural bias argument that perceived low-risk workplace activities and unacceptable psychosocial behaviours were tolerated. The Block projected a form of dissonance that trivialises the importance of certain HSW cognitions. Findings suggest both low order interventions and emerging psychosocial risks at work are socially trivialised in popular culture. Creating awareness of these attitudes may assist agencies to understand how emerging HSW issues are perceived by the viewing audience to potentially counteract a dissonance of views about workplace culture and behaviour in popular media. To that end reality TV audiences have seen it fit to publicly call out certain HSW behaviours at this workplace. These public rebukes support some observations made in this study. The Block therefore serves a useful sociological purpose in understanding HSW cultural exchange at work, and its influence extends beyond commodifiable entertainment.

Contents

1 Introduction: Reality Television Work-Related Activity
and Health, Safety and Wellbeing ... 1
Definitions and Scope ... 2
The Convergence of Reality TV and Construction Work ... 5
The Chapters to Follow and Structure of the Study ... 8
Limitations ... 14
References ... 16

2 Why Is Reality TV Work-Related Activity? ... 19
Reality TV Is Just Entertainment and Not Actual Work Is It Not?: Recent Legal Developments ... 20
Work (Occupational) Health and Safety Legislative Interpretation of Work ... 23
TV Codes of Practice and Standards for Regulation of Reality TV ... 24
The Block Is Work First Followed by Reality TV ... 26
References ... 28

3 The Block 2020 Season 16 and Its Ordinary Participants ... 31
Food (McDonalds), Clothing (Bisley Workwear) and Shelter (Building a Home): What's Maslow's Hierarchy of Needs Got to Do with the Block? ... 37

ix

*Reality TV Manipulation and Audience Interaction
and Concerns*   39
References   41

4 Theoretical Underpinnings for the Data   43
Cultural Risk Theory/Cultural Theory of Risk   44
Applying Trivialisation Dissonance to Cultural Theory of Risk   46
References   48

5 Method and Measurement   51
Methodological Approach   52
Research Design Justification   54
Rationale for the Approach to the Coding   55
References   57

6 Results and Discussion   59
Introduction   60
Part A: Typologies 1,2 and 3   61
  First Typology: Skylarking/Inattention/Lax PPE   61
*Electrical Fires Are Not Entertainment: What's So Funny
About Episode 23 (2:50–5:30)?*   66
Lax PPE: Harden up Mate and Man It out George!   68
This Is Reality TV so Harden up Mate!   71
Inadvertence and Inconsistent Signage Observance   75
Site Hazards: Clutter, Mess and Poor Food Hygiene Examples   80
*Clutter and Housekeeping: It's All Fun and Games Until
Harry Breaks a Bone on Uneven Ground*   81
Luke the Chippy or Luke the Chef?   83
Part B: Typologies 4,5 and 6   84
  *Intangible Considerations: Social Environment, Culture
and Psychosocial Concerns*   84
Portrayal of Alcohol at Work   103
*Gendered Language and Attribute Stereotype Description
and Communication: "Words, Words, Words"—Matter;
Don't They?*   109
Various Psychosocial Hazards   112
Aggression   113

Stress and Antagonism: Dirty Rotten Mongrel	116
Fat Shaming	117
Fat or Lazy?	120
Fatigue and Wearing It as Badge of Honour	121
A Culture of Stress	123
References	145

7 **Conclusion: Is It Just Me Being a Killjoy and What Are the Public Optics?** 151
   References 158

Index 159

About the Author

Trajce Cvetkovski is Discipline Leader and Senior Lecturer in Occupational Health, Safety and Environmental Management at Australian Catholic University. He holds a Ph.D. (Political Science) from the University of Queensland. Trajce is also a work-relations lawyer and was a work health and safety prosecutor from 2006 to 2018. He specialises in regulation and compliance concerning physical and psychosocial hazards and risks. His teaching and research interests are wide and include OHS law in practice and the representation of OHS in popular culture. He is the author of *Copyright and Popular Media: Liberal Villains* and *Technological Change* (Palgrave Macmillan) and *The Pop Music Idol and the Spirit of Charisma* (Palgrave Macmillan). Trajce is also the producer of the globally successful *WhyWork*® podcast.

ABBREVIATIONS

ACMA	Australian Communications and Media Authority
CoP	Code of Practice
CRT/CTR	Cultural Risk Theory/Cultural Theory of risk
CT	Cultural Theory
DIY	Do-it-Yourself
Hi-Viz	High Visibility
OCD	Obsessive Compulsive Disorder OCD
OHS	Occupational Health and Safety
PCBU	Person Conducting a Business or Undertaking
PPE	Personal Protective Equipment
RA	Risk Analysis
SWA	Safe Work Australia
TV	Television
WHS Act	Work Health and Safety Act
WHSW or HSW	Workplace Health, Safety and Wellbeing

List of Figures

Fig. 6.1	Tangible issues—48 episodes where work was conducted	60
Fig. 6.2	Tangible issues—averaged per episode (48 episodes where work was conducted)	61
Fig. 6.3	Intangible issues—48 episodes where work was conducted	104
Fig. 6.4	Intangible issues—averaged per episode (48 episodes where work was conducted)	104

List of Tables

Table 3.1	Season 16 The Block Couples	34
Table 6.1	Season 16 (2020) The Block Observation: Code Book for Typologies 1, 2 & 3	85
Table 6.2	Season 16 (2020) The Block Observation: Code Book for Typologies 4, 5 & 6	124

CHAPTER 1

Introduction: Reality Television Work-Related Activity and Health, Safety and Wellbeing

Abstract How popular culture shapes attitudes towards workplace health, safety and wellbeing (WHSW) has received little attention in the literature. The chapter provides the rationale for examining whether some aspects of workers' HSW are trivialised (if at all) in the Australian construction and renovation reality television show, The Block. Adopting an observational approach, the entire Season 16 (2020) ($n = 50$ episodes) was critically reviewed to assess the level of trivialisation of both identifiable hazards and low order controls. The observations focussed on workplace activities generally perceived or deemed as not high risk or not likely dangerous in the traditional WHSW sense. This introductory chapter sets the scene for the chapters to follow and provides the structure of the study. It also provides definitions that inform the research and provides the scope for the undertaking. It also presents a justification for exploring the convergence of reality TV and construction work and identifies the study's limitations.

Keywords Reality TV · The Block · Trivialisation · Work health safety wellbeing · Psychosocial hazards

© The Author(s), under exclusive license to Springer Nature Switzerland AG 2024
T. Cvetkovski, *Reality Television and the Art of Trivialising Work Health, Safety and Wellbeing*,
https://doi.org/10.1007/978-3-031-64098-8_1

The aim of this undertaking is to assess the extent to which work health, safety and wellbeing (WHSW) considerations are trivialised on television (TV). In particular, it is concerned with the reality TV programme, The Block. Reality TV as a genre plays a core feature in media and cultural studies, but there has not been any research on the impact of reality TV on workplace safety culture, or how HSW issues are portrayed in popular media. A possible explanation is that a connection has not been made first, with the role of the contestant as a *worker*, and second, the televised show as a *workplace*.

This research remedies this deficiency and demonstrates contestant participants on The Block are workers who perform activities at a workplace. The work-related activities are concerned with construction, building and renovation work; and specifically, participants engage in what are seemingly routine or ordinary everyday life activities; namely housing construction and domestic or home dwelling renovations.[1] A sociological framework has been created to explore the nexus between reality TV and HSW at work.

DEFINITIONS AND SCOPE

For this investigation, HSW at the workplace means the promotion and facilitation of a healthy physical and psychosocial work environment for continuous improvement in worker welfare (WHO, 2020). Health and safety considerations require the implementation of robust procedures to minimise psychosocial and physical harm at work. Wellbeing conceptualises the intangible dimension of workplace strategies designed to promote positive workplace environments and is otherwise referred to as a salutogenic approach (Simons & Baldwin, 2021). International Standard *ISO 6385:2016* expands on this understanding to incorporate notions of a sustainable internal state of physical and cognitive satisfaction provided by the system of work in which the worker is placed (2016). The central question guiding this research asks to what extent (if at all) are aspects of HSW trivialised on this show.

Trivialisation is defined as the act of making something seem less important and serious (Australian Oxford Dictionary, 2004). The topic

---

[1] As supported by legal developments, the claim that contestants are workers is extended to other genres such as cooking shows, however the study is limited to construction work reality TV.

of Chapter 4, Simon et al. (1995) refers to trivialisation as a mode of reduction or diminution in the value placed on something of importance to the point of dissonance. Attitudes or actions are trivialised when the dissonance does not involve highly important cognitive elements (Simon et al., 1995).

Workers or employers may be regarded as possessing casual or indifferent attitudes to certain workplace activities if engaged in risk trivialisation behaviour. Such behaviour may be conscious (deliberate) or unconscious (inadvertent). In other words, some health and safety issues are deemed so low risk that they are hardly worth worrying about and not important despite the possibility of liability, contravention or violation of a regulation or industry standard compliance requirement. Trivialisation devalues workplace culture because if perceived risks and the likelihood of harm from those risks are deemed not serious or significant, then they must be culturally of less value in terms of HSW. Such attitudes create a path to trivialisation dissonance because workers deem some activities as being less important cognitively, or as irrelevant life concerns (Simon et al., 1995). The concern with trivialisation dissonance is that irrespective of how risk is perceived, the duty to ensure HSW at work is an objective question of fact and law. From a cultural perspective, the greater the understanding of risk through adequate or accepted best practices (Wilkins, 2011), the more likely an organisation possesses a higher level of risk maturity.

The subject of discussion below, tangible or physical examples of trivialisation generally concerns poor site management (Sharma & Gupta, 2019) which might include untidy sites, clutter and casual observation of mandatory signage to indicate workers must wear required personal protective equipment (PPE). The risk is perceived as minor or inconsequential if compliance is not as rigid or onerous as, for example the erection of scaffolding when working at height.

A more vexed and complex arena of workplace trivialisation which is psychosocial in nature is difficult to measure using traditional risk management knowledge. Risk trivialisation here might occur when a person makes a general casual remark about a worker with "extra padding" not feeling the cold in the office.[2] Such a remark made at work has been held at law to be insensitive and disparaging; irrespective of the fact the

---

[2] Bastoni v ORC International (2019) is discussed later.

person who said these words did not intend to cause hurt and humiliation. Similarly trivialisation might occur when a mental health disorder such as Obsessive Compulsive Disorder (OCD) is introduced into popular culture to jokingly describe personal preference regarding the arrangement of belongings or tidying a room (Robinson et al., 2019); or as was the case in the first episode of The Block, flippant remarks made about obsessively labelling a kitchen pantry.[3] Such communications are capable of being disrespectful and potentially not inclusive in the workplace. So casualised has society become about this mental health disorder, that the International OCD Foundation provides guidance to sufferers on how to cope with societal misinformation about this mental illness. It has had to publish "Dos" and "Don'ts" when responding to OCD jokes (IOCDF, 2024).

The law defines a psychosocial hazard as something that arises or is related to a work environment, and this includes workplace interactions and behaviours where acts or omissions at that workplace may cause psychological harm.[4] Psychosocial hazards are broad-spectrum and can create harm through a worker's experience of stress, anxiety, and tension. This could occur from a variety of activities including stress fatigue from poor work design. Physiological responses such as increased heart rate due to work demands or conflict at work are also connected to psychosocial hazards capable of creating harm. In this context, the Code defines a psychological injury as a disorder or illness that includes a range of recognised cognitive, emotional, physical and behavioural symptoms (2022: 5). The nature of these hazards suggests they could be classed as intangible hazards. For example, stress triggered by bullying fatigue, confrontation and aggression may manifest differently from one person to another over time and as a continuum.

---

[3] Refer to Table 6.2.

[4] Legislative definitions are generally universal. The above explanation has been drawn from Queensland's *Work Health and Safety Regulation 2011* and Managing the risk of psychosocial hazards at work Code of Practice 2022 (Code).

THE CONVERGENCE OF REALITY TV AND CONSTRUCTION WORK

The central proposition guiding this research is that normative guides as to how people behave at the workplace are blurred through the tele-real lens. Data obtained from The Block supports a cultural bias argument (Douglas & Wildavsky, 1982) that perceived low-risk workplace activities and individual behaviours are not only tolerated but at times encouraged, tacitly or directly. As the level of HSW awareness of these activities is perceived as being low, individuals are less motivated to prioritise their importance. The social structures and individual agency created in the show interact to shape contestants' behaviours, dispositions and preferences about perceived risks because their experiences and interactions encompass a set of deeply ingrained, often unconscious, habits, tastes, and ways of thinking. The negative consequence of such attitudes can be regarded as a form of dissonance (Festinger, 1957). To dilute the importance of safety signs, tolerating tiredness or working in untidiness are behaviours akin to convincing oneself that certain risks posed are not severe. That is, such considerations or habits do not really matter because they do not symbolise serious and therefore, actual harm.

The subject of discussion below, what is the likelihood that a tiny splinter penetrating the palm of one's hand will lead to surgical intervention? Should the worker simply "Man Up"? It is this discrepancy between what individuals know to be important for their health and safety and subsequent actions or beliefs that may cause mental conflict downplaying the importance of certain behaviours. This can lead to potentially risky or harmful behaviour as individuals may not take necessary precautions or actions to safeguard their health and wellbeing. Accordingly, this research is concerned with the intersection of various conflicting symbols, and the semiotic structures created through risk trivialisation dissonance. The communicative acts presented on this show are powerful because consumers are not only motivated to learn about on-trend home design, they are vociferous on social media about how symbols of HSW are transmitted. Recent complaints to authorities by the audience concerning psychosocial hazards and the wellbeing of contestants on The Block signify audience agency and social investment in popular media creation and interpretation (Bell, 2010).

What happens in renovation reality shows does imitate quite reasonably and practically what happens in the real world. While shows such as *Married First Site, Beauty and the Geek, Bachelor* or *Farmer wants are Wife* provide affective entertainment whether it is for shock value or just sheer spectacle of watching ordinary persons consenting to cultural experiments, The Block adds significant intrinsic worth to important things in life such as creating a tangible good such as a beautiful home or in other words, significant real estate. The work being performed is socio-economically serious and is measured in terms of commodifiable value. There is nothing pointless or banal about the objective of the show as the contestants are serious contenders and not wannabe reality TV stars (Cvetkovski, 2015). This is because the true celebrities or stars of the show are the multi-million dollar houses that are transformed into an object of (unattainable) desire. The audience is genuinely fascinated by the true worth of the creations as is evidenced in the final two episodes of the show which are devoted to the spectacle of the auction process.

So socially relevant is the content on this renovation show that politicians have opinions about it. Consider the following extract by Senator Lisa Singh (as the Honourable member then was) (2012):

> *There is an obligation on reality DIY renovation TV shows to highlight the dangers associated with asbestos. Last year, a contestant of such a show said publicly that there had been an expectation participants would work in a dusty environment and remove their masks when they were required to speak to camera.*
>
> *Such shows are designed to inspire people to renovate which is why, in a bid to promote their products, prominent hardware companies form partnerships with such shows. But failing to advise viewers of the dangers associated with asbestos, especially when it has been identified and safely removed 'off camera', is deplorable. In inspiring people to renovate, there is an obligation to ensure Australians are aware renovation is not always as simple as it may be made to look. There is a need to ensure this third wave of painful and unnecessary asbestos-related deaths does not continue in decades to come.*
>
> *Since being lobbied, Channel Nine has announced it will include reference to having conducted an asbestos audit on its popular renovation program, The Block. The Executive Producer said viewers would also be advised to be aware of asbestos and seek advice on its presence and removal before undertaking renovations.*

The show's impact on housing construction work and subsequent inspiration is endearing, but when the show attracts controversial media attention, the content extends beyond the tele-real spectacle of the auction. The Block was recently criticised over representations made about controversial stone products. Headlines such as "Blockbuster renovation show The Block has been slammed by lawyers, the building industry and health experts over one segment" (Evans, 2023) echo concerns made by the Hon. Singh in 2012 about asbestos and renovation. Friedlander (2023) went further by exclaiming "The Block has been plunged into controversy for promoting products that contain a substance being referred to as the new asbestos". Remarkably according to the article, Channel 9 defended the show's use of the particular brand of stone because that particular product was deemed not dangerous per the Regulator's definition, and in any event, "no stone was cut onsite" (Frielander, 2023). Furthermore, the show's host Cam Scott explained to viewers "the products had 'minimal silica' — like natural — that naturally occurs in beach sand or something like that — so it's very safe" (Frielander, 2023). As reported by the media, there was union push back over The Block's "promotion of engineered stone benchtops" (Frielander, 2023). These concerns prima facie elevate the show's status beyond that of mere entertainment and interest in realty. They are evidence of socio-political, legal and general national WHSW interest.

Singh's passage is significant for two reasons. The first is that as The Block inspires the audience to aspire to renovate through the consumption of goods and services it also has an obligation to educate its viewers about the dangers of this undertaking. Secondly, the passage alerts the reader to the conditions of the contestants. The reader is reminded these people are not "wannabe antitalented" reality TV attention seekers (Cvetkovski, 2015). Rather they are workers undertaking potentially hazardous work.

Singh's observations are prescient. Made some eight years before, Season 16, it is worth querying why PPE was not used when Luke from House 4 (H4)[5] was observed emptying an item of plant used for vacuuming dust. Asbestos nanoparticles concerns aside, what was Luke potentially inhaling? The Western Australian Government, unremarkably, alerts people who renovate homes about renovation dust; and provides occupational guidance around dust and other airborne contaminants (2012):

---

[5] (E10: 14:59).

> *Dust, and fibres, that may be generated from renovation activities can be irritating to your eyes, nose and throat, while some can cause your skin to itch. Very fine dust and fibres can be breathed deep into your lungs and cause breathing problems if you are sensitive to these dusts and fibres. Some renovation dusts and fibres are hazardous when they contain asbestos, respirable crystalline silica or lead.*

The point made here is not that the bin may have contained hazardous nanoparticles[6] but rather, why was PPE not being worn in this very real-world setting? The proceeding section sets the scene for the chapters to follow.

THE CHAPTERS TO FOLLOW AND STRUCTURE OF THE STUDY

This chapter sets the scene for the chapters to follow. Chapter 2 briefly provides a justification for considering The Block as a place where a business or undertaking is being performed. It relies on doctrinal developments in the form of case law and builds on statutory WHS developments to validate the observation that a reality show is a workplace first, and entertainment in the form of commercial free-to-air reality TV programming, second. In other words, those caught on camera are at premises in which workers, employees, others as individuals, are persons defined by law. This definition is applied throughout the entire season to not only contestants but also tradespeople, delivery staff, caterers, film crew, sales representatives and all other contractors permitted to enter the site. In other words, a specific work activity was being conducted on that site, and its activity was being documented for commercial exploitation. If it is accepted that work was being conducted (which clearly it was), then there is no reason why The Block site would be viewed any differently than that of any other construction site. It was a televised construction site and not an artificial show filmed in the studio. For example, several signs were depicted to indicate to the world at large about warning unauthorised persons to keep out. Signs mandated employees must be inducted and individuals such as visitors authorised to enter the site, were to report to the Office. Anyone else not authorised to enter the site would be deemed,

---

[6] Although in the previous episode, a concern by a supervisor about possible cement sheeting/asbestos was raised (refer to Table 6.1).

therefore, to be a trespasser. The purpose of Chapter 2 is to emphasise the contestant participants described in the proceeding chapters should be viewed as workers by virtue of their activities. This chapter also sets the scene for observations about activities that support the central argument that certain cultural risks were trivialised.

Chapter 3 introduces the 10 contestants of The Block within the broader reality TV framework setting. On the one hand, critics may accuse the show of promoting consumerism as homeowners aspire to prioritise aesthetics and resale through profit value over functionality and sustainability. This is a valid argument given the pivotal role the judges play and the emphasis on high-end finishes and on-trend designs which contribute to a culture of excess, rather than promoting responsible and sustainable home improvement practices. However, the show does extend the aesthetic of art to reality because it also explores a primary human need to ensure stability and security through homeownership followed by aspirational desires. To this end, this chapter relies on Maslow's theoretical framework to support the observation that safety is also a motivating factor whether that be financial, psychological or physical (Wilkins, 2011). The show promotes the notion that shelter is essential for economic survival. This primary safety need is vital for wellbeing of the contestants. That is, the contestants are essentially aspiring to create foundations for building a better family life and the fact all the couples built five glorious homes together did represent a sense of community. This primary desire is a clear motivating factor for competing on this show. There are less clear tangible factors as to why people would enter several other reality TV genres, but The Block is grounded on a pivotal need for not only survival, but self-actualisation thereby contributing to overall health and wellbeing (Maslow, 1943).

Two theoretical underpinnings which guide this research are explained in Chapter 4. The first is the cultural theory of risk perception. In Risk and Culture (1982) Douglas and Wildavsky introduced the cultural theory to risk analysis (RA), and of significance is how attitudes, beliefs and behaviours are shaped through the social construction of risk. Risk perception informs risk analysis and a central argument of Douglas and Wildavsky is that cultural biases determine which hazards pose high or low risk. Data obtained from the show empirically validates this cultural bias argument in which relations are prescribed.

This theory is applied to The Block because wider moral questions are posed about categorising workplace practices as social discourse. To the individual, what is the value of PPE or what does it matter if signage is ignored; especially as administrative control is so low on the order of hierarchy of control and elimination? What norms have materially transgressed by social groups to warrant risky behaviour or poor cultural practices at work? Simply because jokes are made in poor taste, archaic, gendered language is used, or alcohol is permitted on a construction site does not mean engagement in risky or unacceptable workplace conduct. It may simply mean those engaging in these behaviours do not place highly important cognitive elements (Simon et al., 1995) to these activities. It is contended risks are socially created to serve the social relations of those perceiving and analysing them. In this context, CT is useful in providing a critical framework for analysis of how hazards are interpreted, identified and assessed, and what normative value is placed on whether there is any likelihood of risk attached to a hazard (Douglas, 1992). As a form of collective conscience, CT of risk perception is applied to the subsequent influence of specific cultural biases in this reality show because CT assists in understanding how specific social groups interact at workplaces in order to determine their values and outlooks about conventional and emerging risks (Douglas, 1992).

Introduced at the outset, the second theoretical underpinning guiding this study is trivialisation as a mode of dissonance from any consistency in subject matter which reduces the viewer to some cognitive dissonance (Simon et al., 1995). This process refers to the act of downplaying or underestimating the severity or likelihood of potential dangers or negative outcomes associated with a particular action or situation. It is a mode of cognitive bias where individuals or groups minimise the significance of risks, leading to increased risk-taking behaviour and a neglect of necessary safety precautions (Festinger, 1957). Combined the theory of CT of risk perception and risk trivialisation dissonance are used to explain the level of inconsistencies involving cognitions central to WHSW. The result of this dissonance is to reduce the activities to trivialisation because they are not seen as risky or unacceptable actions (Simon et al., 1995). These theories assist in explaining why the individual on The Block potentially reduced the importance of certain elements of WHSW.

Chapter 5 sets out the methods and measurement adopted in the study. The design of the research was exploratory in nature as it was used to examine values about certain workplace activities commonly clustered or perceived to be ranked at the lower end of risk and therefore less dangerous or harmful (if at all). An observational design was applied since the purpose was to attempt to detect and code patterns of activities, conduct and behaviours by repeatedly watching the entire season. The intention was to identify potential activities, analyse the content and evaluate specific themes particularised in six broad typologies. Adopting this observational approach, Season 16 (2020) ($n = 50$ episodes) was critically reviewed on three separate occasions to assess the level of trivialisation of identifiable hazards and controls.

The following propositions were tested: (1) onsite skylarking, inattention and lax PPE usage were tolerated or downplayed in certain instances; (2) safety signage compliance was inconsistent throughout the season; (3) site untidiness and occasional hygiene issues were observed; (4) onsite consumption and promotion of alcohol appeared to be normalised; (5) antiquated gendered language or stereotyping was used; and (6) potential exposure to various psychosocial hazards was accepted or inadequately addressed on occasion. A cultural theory of risk perception was applied to events or scenes to identify specific and repeated instances of trivialisation dissonance relating to the above typologies.

Chapter 6 presents the results of the observational study. The data presented in Figs. 6.1–6.4 should be construed as a systems evaluation in light of the observed interactions. For example, any inferences drawn by the observations that a cluttered site might likely attract an inadvertent slip, trip and fall injury are made in the spirit of the design approach and are not to be considered as accusatory in nature.[7]

The observations have been made to detect any potential for mishap, mischief or unintended consequences in relation to low order or perceived low-risk exposures to hazards at work. Similarly, any observation about reference to alcohol is not concerned with being affected by alcohol. Rather, the observations are concerned with the culture of alcohol in a sociological context because as demonstrated in this show (and other reality TV programming), the drug, alcohol does play a significant role in Western culture. It is especially important for this study because as observed by Roche et al. (2020) the workplace rituals of alcohol are often couched within the positively valued Australian ideals of mateship and work ethic and as such usually refer to forms of bonding and solidarity. The authors conclude on the one hand alcohol is integral to the Australian

---

[7] However, contestant workers in Season 16 (and other seasons) were reported in the media to have received physical injuries which are commonly described as slips, trips and falls. The exposure to these hazards was tangible.

way of life but that it is also a major contributor to preventable illness and death, and affects overall wellbeing; especially for young people leaving school and entering the workforce (Roche et al., 2020). The subject of this chapter, the semiotics of alcohol is omnipotent.

Tables 6.1 and 6.2 present a running sheet of observed events for each episode, with each event clustered in one of the six typologies described above. Figures are provided to indicate rates of occurrence. In addition to this, analyses of specific noteworthy events are provided. Three key themes emerged. First, there was a perception that administrative and lower-wrung interventions were inconsistently applied and monitored during the season. Secondly, a culture of alcohol at work was normalised and the imagery at times was confusing in terms of when work finished and alcohol consumption commenced. Thirdly, psychosocial hazards awareness was either inadequate or undervalued. Other less overt themes emerged, details of which are examined in this chapter but the data supports a cultural bias argument that certain perceived low-risk workplace activities and unacceptable behaviours were tolerated, ignored or not comprehensively addressed.

This data gave the viewer the impression The Block projected a form of dissonance that trivialised the importance of certain HSW cognitions. If this has occurred, then any conflict or inconsistency between workers' beliefs, attitudes, or behaviours regarding health, safety, and wellbeing and what is reasonably expected of workers, at the workplace, should be addressed. A tendency to downplay or underestimate the significance of certain health-related concerns should not be encouraged or accepted in any setting. This observation extends beyond the stars of the show, and applies to persons not directly related to the worksite. For example, why did some visiting real estate agents wear Hi-Viz vests during site inspections and others did not in circumstances where that type of PPE was required to be worn in light of mandatory PPE signage (see E11)? That is, did all visitors report to the office and were they instructed to wear Hi-Viz? Perception and consistency do matter in the promotion of workplace culture.

Exploring some of these behaviours also raises questions about the motivation for change for continuous improvement at the workplace. When someone downplays health risks concerned for example, with poor food hygiene, they might feel less motivated to make positive changes such as hand sanitisation. Since Covid, the stress and anxiety around this simple practice has become increasingly heightened. Minimising risk trivialisation could address the internal conflict that can arise from poor practice thereby reducing stress and anxiety around ambiguity. Thus people might use cognitive dissonance to justify not washing hands because others may not at work or as there may not be any washing facilities, the poor workplace practices become normalised. Similarly, such cognitive dissonance might apply in circumstances where the worker downplays the importance of wearing PPE because they have convinced themselves by virtue of their experience they were in control of the undertaking. This is a reasonable observation in light of the fact some of the participants in Table 3.1 were experienced in carpentry, plumbing and electrical work. Be that as it may, many participants were not tradespeople and the viewing audience observed all activity at face value. The author accepts it is arguable that some observations coded in this research can be reasonably explained and justified, and some challenged or even construed as misinterpreted or misguided because they were incidental or one-off events. But it would be difficult to justify how any construction site would approve a worker (Tam H5) replete with Hi-Viz and with cement mixer truck in situ nearby, and holding on to a glass of what appears to be white wine. Similarly in the same scene, a labourer is seen clasping onto what appears to be a glass bottle of Corona beer whilst concrete is being set in the evening (refer to Table 4, E37). Perhaps the glass bottle was a non-alcoholic beverage, but the image was open to conjecture.

The conclusion in Chapter 7 is that the findings suggest both low order interventions and emerging psychosocial risks at work are socially trivialised in popular cultural settings. Practical applications from this research could result in creating an awareness of these attitudes which in turn may assist agencies to understand how emerging HSW issues are perceived by the viewing audience. Potentially counteracting a dissonance of views about workplace culture and behaviour in popular media could include encouraging workers to accept trivialisation creep may dilute the importance of certain WHSW cognitions. The study creates awareness about contrasting beliefs such as downplaying the tendency to diminish the significance of warning signage, PPE or use of antiquated or insensitive language. People should be encouraged to confront the inconsistency and make positive changes that align with acceptable beliefs and actions. The alternative is to tolerate risk trivialisation but in doing so people risk negative outcomes.

Limitations

It is acknowledged that limitations affect this study. An obvious contention is whether the interpretation of an image depicted was objectively accurate. Just because for example a worker was not wearing high visibility clothing (Hi-Viz) at that captured moment does not mean there was overall non-compliance of this basic requirement at the workplace. And just because a can of beer was placed on the set does not mean alcohol was consumed at that point. However, the viewer is entitled to query these images from a cultural risk perspective as the argument raised in this study is that the show is a workplace first and foremost. As set out above, the research was designed to be exploratory given the changing landscape in which work is conceptualised in advanced capitalist society. It is emphasised the scope of this study is neither prosecutorial in nature nor is it a polemic against The Block or any other reality TV generally. It is concerned with perceptions of a safe system of work within a broader rubric for the continuous improvement of health, safety and wellbeing.

The coded observations are not designed to elementise factual ingredients for the formulation of a potential WHS offence. Instead, observations have been made to gain a better understanding of the system of work designed on The Block. According to Dekker, "For progress on safety, organisations must monitor and understand the reasons behind the gap between procedures and practice" (2003: 233). Dekker claims safety results from people being skilful at judging when and how (and when not to) adapt procedures to local circumstances. In other words, organisations must consider the support to ensure people's skill are reasonably and practicably maintained (Dekker, 2003). The focus on specific occurrences in this study is presented in their wider context where elements of work are designed to interact as part of a holistic consideration of unresolved issues on this specific reality TV show filmed in a particularly anxious global period—COVID-19.

In the context of a sociotechnical system approach, this study does explore, legitimately, cultural perceptions about how some aspects of work are performed on the show. For example, an observation about not wearing eye protection in circumstances where a worker is using an item of plant that could produce hazardous particles (wood shavings) is clearly confusing to the viewer. This is because the instruction manual expressly states in bold "**Use personal protective equipment. Always wear eye**

protection"[8] when operating a Makita cordless planer. This is an example of risk trivialisation dissonance and the concerns raised are made validly and in the spirit of academic enquiry because the optics of such are scene are questionable and worth interrogating.[9]

Similarly, observations about dangling leads or cluttered work spaces may be criticised by the reader as being pedantic or excessive. They have been observed not because an incident occurred from a dangling power cable, but rather in the context that there may be a perceived exposure to risk as a result of messy or cluttered sites. A systems approach to WHSW requires consideration of the entire system of work from extremely high-risk activity (work on the edge of a six-metre roof) to slips, trips and falls caused by a messy site. Integrated system safety requires hazards and risks detection across the entire system and should be adaptive, for guidance on good work design systems, PCBUs or employers could consult ISO Standard 6385. By way of illustration, it is no secret *The Block* is fast-paced and hectic and this adds to the obvious drama. Therefore, OHS professionals on the show would especially need to be mindful of system variability and scrutinise the likelihood of loose cables and messy floors in a frenetic environment. Detailed design of work organisation, tasks, environment, jobs, equipment, and work spaces could be achieved by having regard to the scope and nature of the show's scope of works as construction site contain within a reality TV deadline.

The Block is a very entertaining reality TV show and it should be recognised as a complex sociotechnical system in which humans work. Its appeal to contestants and the audience lies in the dream of fulfilling a human need; the provision of shelter; even if it is of the highest aspirational order. But the demands of those participating in the undertaking are intense and potential errors in best practice are visible. The findings demonstrate this TV genre contains certain questionable and unacceptable workplace practices that do not adequately promote the importance of all HSW considerations.

---

[8] Refer to Makita Cordless Planer Instruction Manual for Model KP001G at p. 3.

[9] As corroborated by significant media attention, viewers have successfully made complaints to authorities about trivialisation of safe work practices in TV commercials because the imagery was deemed unacceptable in terms of best work practices. The subject of discussion below, a concerned viewer was justified in the slapstick portrayal of foreign particles escaping into the air as portrayed in the Bisley Workwear commercial.

REFERENCES

Australian Oxford Dictionary. (2004). Oxford University Press.
Bastoni v ORC International (2019) FWC 38.
Bell, C. E. (2010). *American idolatry: Celebrity, commodity and reality television.* McFarland.
Cvetkovski, T. (2015). *The pop music idol and the spirit of charisma: Reality television talent shows in the digital economy of hope Palgrave Macmillan.* https://doi.org/10.1057/9781137494467
Dekker, S. (2003). Failure to adapt or adaptations that fail: Contrasting models on procedures and safety applied. *Ergonomics, 34,* 233–238.
Douglas, M., & Wildavsky, A. (1982). *Risk and culture: An essay on the selection of technological and environmental dangers.* University of California Press.
Douglas, P. M. (1992). *Risk and blame: Essays in cultural theory.* Routledge.
Evans, J. (2023). *The Block on blast over controversial stone products.* https://www.news.com.au/entertainment/tv/the-block-on-blast-over-controversial-stone-products/news-story/2893dd859ee51eb58a6493a74e203c66?amp
Festinger, L. (1957). *A theory of cognitive dissonance.* Row, Peterson.
Frielander, M. (2023). *The block slammed for promoting stone products containing a substance linked to an incurable disease that's killing tradies: 'The new asbestos'.* https://www.dailymail.co.uk/tvshowbiz/article-12659909/The-Block-slammed-promoting-stone-products-containing-substance-linked-incurable-disease-thats-killing-tradies-new-asbestos.html
International OCD Foundation. (2024). https://iocdf.org/
ISO 6385:2016. (2021). *Ergonomics principles in the design of work systems.* https://www.iso.org/standard/63785.html
Makita Cordless Planer Instruction Manual for Model KP001G makita.com
Managing the Risk of Psychosocial Hazards at Work Code of Practice. (2022). https://www.worksafe.qld.gov.au/__data/assets/pdf_file/0025/104857/managing-the-risk-of-psychosocial-hazards-at-work-code-of-practice.pdf
Maslow, A. H. (1943). A theory of human motivation. *Psychological Review, 50,* 370–396.
Robinson, P., Turk, D., Jilka, S., & Cella, M. (2019). Measuring attitudes towards mental health using social media: Investigating stigma and trivialisation. *Social Psychiatry and Psychiatric Epidemiology, 54*(1), 51–58.
Roche, A. M., Bywood, P., Freeman T., Pidd, K., Borlagdan, J., & Trifonoff, A. (2009). *The social context of alcohol use in Australia.* National Centre for Education and Training on Addiction.
Roche, A., Chapman, J., Duraisingam, V., Phillips, B., Finnane, J., Pidd, K. (2020). Construction workers' alcohol use, knowledge, perceptions of risk and workplace norms. *Drug and Alcohol Review, 39*(7), 941–949.

Sharma, S., & Gupta, A. (2019). Risk identification and management in construction projects: Literature review. *International Journal of Humanities: Arts and Social Sciences, 5,* 224–231.

Simon, L., Greenberg, J., & Brehm, J. (1995). Trivialization: The forgotten mode of dissonance reduction. *Journal of Personality and Social Psychology, 68*(2), 247. https://doi.org/10.1037/0022-3514.68.2.247

Simons, G., & Baldwin, D. S. (2021). A critical review of the definition of 'wellbeing' for doctors and their patients in a post Covid-19 era. *International Journal of Social Psychiatry, 67*(8), 984–991. https://doi.org/10.1177/00207640211032259

Singh, L. (2012). *Asbestos killed this man: Are you safe?* https://www.mamamia.com.au/asbestos-warning-for-home-renovators-as-the-block-is-back-on-tv/

Spitfire. (2024). *Original instructions operating and maintenance manual,* L-L 283.01-SW Spitfire Australia.

Wilkins, J. (2011). Construction workers' perceptions of health and safety training programmes. *Construction Management and Economics, 29*(10), 1017–1026. https://doi.org/10.1080/01446193.2011.633538

Work Health and Safety Act and Regulation 2011. (Queensland)

World Health Organization. (2020). *Healthy workplace model for action.* World Health Organization.

CHAPTER 2

Why Is Reality TV Work-Related Activity?

Abstract This chapter considers recent legal developments in the field of reality TV. It also examines OHS work (occupational) health and safety legislative interpretation of work including changes to TV codes of practice and standards for regulation of reality TV. The chapter provides a justification for considering The Block as a place where a business or undertaking is being performed. It relies on doctrinal developments in the form of case law and builds on statutory developments to validate the observation that a reality show is a workplace first, and entertainment in the form of commercial TV programming, second. The purpose of this chapter is to emphasise the contestant participants described in the proceeding chapters should be viewed as workers by virtue of their activities. It also sets the scene for observations about activities that support the central argument that certain cultural risks were trivialised.

Keywords Reality TV · Workplace laws · The Block · Code of Conduct · Media

© The Author(s), under exclusive license to Springer Nature Switzerland AG 2024
T. Cvetkovski, *Reality Television and the Art of Trivialising Work Health, Safety and Wellbeing*,
https://doi.org/10.1007/978-3-031-64098-8_2

Reality TV Is Just Entertainment and Not Actual Work Is It Not?: Recent Legal Developments

The socio-legal scope of this research is guided by recent case law and current regulatory developments[1] concerning workplace culture, and harmful behaviours including inappropriate language or jokes, aggression, bullying, fatigue, and alcohol consumption. The justification for defining reality TV as work-related is based on recent legal developments. The first relates to recent case law concerning reality contestants, and the second is the emergence of robust WHSW legislation which is concerned with both physical and psychosocial hazards.

Two recent court decisions support the proposition that networks or producers of these shows potentially possess employer-related duties and owe a duty of care to working individuals. In the *House Rules* (2019) case,[2] the injured person (Prince) sustained a psychological injury as a contestant worker on a building and renovation reality TV show. The format was comparable to that of The Block in that contestants worked as couples against others. Ms Prince was engaged in renovating homes for a chance to win $200,000 and was also paid $1,000 a week in allowances during filming. The worker claimed that once filming began, Channel Seven devised a storyline under which she and her partner were portrayed as the show's villains. Ms Prince alleged the atmosphere at the workplace became hostile and tense. They were shunned by other teams, deliberately isolated, cast in a negative light and generally misrepresented on the show to the public. The worker claimed adverse portrayal led to unhealthy, threatening, aggressive and generally negative social media commentary. The Commission found in favour of Prince who was awarded workers' compensation for psychological injury. Relevantly there existed an employee–employer relationship in circumstances where the reality TV contestant was a worker.

In *My Kitchen Rules*,[3] the aggrieved individual was paid weekly compensation by the Seven Network on a voluntary basis for compensation as an injured worker as the term is used in law. The circumstances, not unlike the House Rules case involved the applicant victim claiming

---

[1] Model *Managing psychosocial hazards at work Code of Practice*, SafeWork Australia July 2022.

[2] *Prince v 7 Network (Operations) Ltd* [2019] NSW WCC313 ("Prince").

[3] *Green v Seven Network (Operations) Limited* [2021].

she had sustained psychological injury over the course of her role on this cooking show. The producers and Seven Network were required to minimise exposure to vilification and bullying experienced during the show.

In the first case, negative and hostile vignettes were aired which led to the audience judging the contestants harshly, including threats of violence on the network website. The matter was further aggravated by the fact the online administrators of the website did not take these communications down but allowed them to remain in the public domain. The network was unsuccessful in arguing that the worker was not an employee. The issue here was not whether a relationship was one of employment, or whether the contestants were deemed workers or sub-contractors, contractors or any other constantly changing definition of a person paid for services pursuant to work and employment legislation. It was whether Channel Seven had a great deal of control over the worker's activities while she was on the show. The aggrieved contestant (and her partner) described difficult working conditions and an overall unpleasant environment where they maintained they felt isolated, harassed and bullied during the filming while attempting to work on the renovations.

The victims in both cases present a workplace that could only be described as toxic. The alleged workplace culture was not only condoned by the producer in the first case but it was aggravated and even encouraged by them according to the worker. The worker claimed once the show was aired and she was portrayed as the villain, she was unable to obtain work and was unable to secure job interviews. The worker generally felt feelings of worthlessness and turned to alcohol. The decision of the arbitrator is compelling (p. 24 see paragraphs [121–124] of the *Prince* 1999 decision):

> There is little doubt the applicant was placed in a hostile environment in the course of her employment…There was editing of the footage from the program in such a selective manner as to portray them in a certain negative light…I find it extraordinary, in the circumstances where the respondent was made aware by the applicant of hateful comments posted on its social media platforms, that it did not take steps to either remove those comments or to close the comments on its own post. The failure to do so represents, in my view, a factor to which the applicant has reacted and which has contributed to her injury.

In *My Kitchen Rules*, the nature of the alleged bullying revolved around control over her phone, distortions of her actions and words by way of production edits, victimisation, bullying and harassment and unfair treatment as the terms are used in law. Of relevance was that Seven's storylines for O'Neill, a married mother of two at the time, included that she had been "sleeping with the enemy", another contestant, and that she was involved in a "sex scandal". These harmful narratives were followed up extensively by the media and the viewers and readers wherein social media allows the audience to participate in the process of vilification. Those in control of the business or undertaking provided the audience with an opportunity to morally judge and as in the case of Prince, condemn the victim for acting villainously.

On any reading of these cases, the factual ingredients support the reason why regulators in Australia have recently approved codes for psychosocial hazards exposure and amendment to work health and safety regulations.[4] This is not to suggest psychological injury was not recognised prior to 2022. It seems legal developments covering psychosocial hazards have been significantly bolstered in recent years to protect individuals engaged in work-related activity. Reality TV shows offer fertile socio-legal opportunities to examine psychological harm against workers because according to these cases, contestants are deemed to be workers or a class of persons with workers' rights.

As set out in the proceeding sections, The Block has not been without its potential psychosocial controversies according to media reports. In 2021 Buaya explained:

> Keith has previously been slammed by viewers as a 'bully'. Last year, he was accused of 'fat-shaming' contestant Daniel Joyce and bitterly butted heads with Harry Pavlou. 'With each season he becomes nastier towards those he's paid to guide through the renovations,' one viewer tweeted.

The same reporter examined the fat shaming incident discussed in Chapter 5, however, it is important to note public interest in the conduct of the above foreperson[5] via social media. Audience perceptions and

---

[4] See for example, amendments to the *Work Health and Safety Regulation 2011 (Qld)* effective 1 April 2023; including the *Code of Practice: Managing the Risk of Psychosocial Hazards at Work*.

[5] Used interchangeably with supervisor.

reactions are pivotal to reality TV appeal, and it seems the show has attracted a significant body of disapproval in relation to the conduct of the forepersons/supervisors.

Work (Occupational) Health and Safety Legislative Interpretation of Work

In the Prince decision, defence counsel for the Channel Seven submitted the concept of "contestant" comes nowhere near that of worker (2019: 15). This argument was squarely rejected by the Commission (at p. 17). Having regard to the relevant workers' compensation legislation and precedent, the tribunal of fact and law categorised the relationship between the parties as that of employee and employer.

Even if the above legal analysis is problematic to some readers, the harmonised Australian law, *Model Work Health and Safety Act 2011*[6] (the Act) is unambiguous in that a person is defined as a *worker* if the person carries out work in any capacity for a person conducting a business or undertaking. Similarly, a *workplace* is a place where work is carried out for a business or undertaking and includes any place where a worker goes, or is likely to be, while at work. There can be no dispute The Block satisfies these elements according to law. It follows then those with a duty of care in order to ensure successful discharge of duties must have regard to the protection of workers and other persons against harm to their health, safety and welfare (see s.3 of the Act for example). This would ordinarily be achieved through the promotion of continuous improvement at the worksite for a safer, healthier workplace and for utmost salutogenic benefit.

As set out in Chapter 1, this research is not concerned with issues relating to determining whether compliance has been achieved or not in the regulatory sense. Rather, it is concerned with facilitation of discussion around consistency in portrayal of certain practices on a reality TV worksite. The law analysed is not being relied on to determine whether events depicted posed serious, overt or immediate risk. Rather the law is being utilised to interrogate whether in the spirit of the law, workers and other persons have been given the highest level of protection against *all*

---

[6] Note the State of Victoria is the only non-member of the harmonised scheme in Australia but its *Occupational Health and Safety Act 2004* embodies similar substantive legal principles.

harm to their health, safety and welfare from all hazards and risks arising from work; including those at the lower end of seriousness (see s3 of the Act). The rationale for this approach is that WHS regulation affects every element of workplace activity in a whole work system setting.

TV Codes of Practice and Standards for Regulation of Reality TV

The Australian Communications and Media Authority (ACMA) has created standards pursuant to the *Broadcasting Services Act 1992*[7] with respect to media industry best practices. The nature of commercial free-to-air regulation and compliance is that it is a co-regulatory scheme. Free-to-air television is regulated by the ACMA and its role inter alia is to regulate media content. It achieves this by ensuring industry codes of practice are not violated in terms of appropriate community standards and safeguards generally with respect to free-to-air commercial content. In keeping with societal norms and values, the arrangement is that industry groups develop codes of practice in consultation with the ACMA and this regulatory body monitors codes and deals with unresolved complaints from viewers and listeners. A curious finding in this research was that until recently, reality TV contestants and their subsequent protection were expressly mentioned in broadcast regulatory instruments. Of interest is the *Free Commercial Television Industry Code of Practice (2015 amended to 2018) (CoP)* which does not make any specific reference to reality TV contestants' rights and how they are to be portrayed or protected.

However, the superseded *Commercial Television Industry Code of Practice—January 2010 (incorporating amendments to July 2013)* did particularise reality TV participation, and it is worth noting the significant change in the current TV CoP compared to the previous code. In the section headed "Proscribed material", the 2010 code provided:

> *1.9 A licensee may not broadcast a program, program promotion, station identification or community service announcement which is likely, in all the circumstances, to:*

---

[7] For example see *Broadcasting Services (Australian Content and Children's Television) Standards 2020*.

1.9.7 present participants in reality television programs in a highly demeaning or highly exploitative manner.
Demeaning: *A depiction or description, sexual in nature, which is a serious debasement of persons, or a group of persons, within a program.*
Exploitative: *Clearly appearing to purposefully debase or abuse a person, or group of persons, for the enjoyment of others, and lacking moral, artistic or other values.*

The *Broadcasting Services Act 1992* expressly prescribes that codes are created by various stakeholders in consultation with the ACMA about matters relating to program content but the design of the code is self-regulatory. This broadcasting law at s.123 is concerned with the development of codes to ensure protection and prevention of exposure to both psychological and physical harm and "such other matters relating to program content as are of concern to the community". Therefore, preventing the broadcasting of material adjudged not to be reflective of "community standards" is an important consideration. It must be asked then, why such a cogent provision would be omitted in revised codes. The previous code clearly and expressly defined proscribed material around reality TV programming.

The focus on reality TV seems to have disappeared from the regulatory landscape which is extraordinary because it is not in keeping with current community focus on greater psychosocial hazards awareness. That is, reference to reality TV was expressly stipulated a decade ago and now the term has been excised. As the Code is not drafted by the ACMA, but rather by stakeholders, it is reasonable to ask why this provision was omitted and why appropriate safeguards for reality TV participants are not in the Code. The subject of discussion below, several complaints against The Block to the authority have been made recently, and even though a Code has no status as subordinate legislation, codes are good lead indicators about determining appropriate community standards for broadcasters. As assessment of code violation is qualitative in kind (based on the force of the complaints), and as there is no meaningful provision in the current Code from which to assess the nature and quality of the broadcast content according to current community standards, it is fair to conclude the rights of reality TV have been diluted from express recognition to no specific recognition. It is arguable whether reality TV participants have implied rights in broadcasting legislation in the premises.

As mentioned, the Block has not been without controversy about questionable psychosocial matters. Widely reported in media, in 2023, the ACMA received 28 complaints or enquiries regarding The Block. The majority of queries and concerns related to allegations of bullying, harassment and promotion of antisocial behaviour between contestants. As Mrad (2023) reports, "it's now been revealed the finale of the controversial show has reportedly been changed following complaints of bullying…It comes after it was revealed the ACMA had been inundated with complaints about the current season of The Block". In this news article an Officer of Channel 9's explained The Block is an unrivalled powerhouse on Australian television. The fact that more than 40% of the country has tuned into this series is a phenomenal achievement' (in Mrad, 2023). This observation alone indicates the show has the potential to shape attitudes and beliefs about workplace culture. If it did not, then the audience would not feel compelled to complain to an authority.

As the nature of media regulation is self-regulatory, the ACMA will only intervene if the matter is not resolved by Channel 9. On the one hand, 28 complaints are a significant number with respect to respect psychosocial matters, but there is no specific code provision from which to assess the merit of the complaints. In the circumstances, it is difficult to construe whether any substantive decision will be made. However, the significant symbolic gesture made by the audience should not be socially undervalued.

THE BLOCK IS WORK FIRST FOLLOWED BY REALITY TV

The final reason for determining *The Block* is a work-related activity is concerned with the COVID-19 pandemic. Proof for this assertion is that the show was spared the strict lockdowns because it was engaging in building and construction services (Victoria State Government, 2020). Despite the chaos of 2020, the show was finalised as it was classified as an essential workplace first, and entertainment second. (Consider the 2020 suspension of *The Masked Singer* also filmed in Melbourne because it was not essential work.)

In 2020, the pandemic tested the resilience of the entire globe. It became patently clear the disruptive and potentially catastrophic economic effects affected every aspect of work. The Block was filmed in Melbourne, the capital of Victoria and its laws and policies concerning Covid were the most stringent in Australia. This stringent approach to the pandemic gained international attention. As construction work was deemed essential work by the government, the business or undertaking of the Block was the construction of dwellings. Accordingly, the show was permitted to continue where several other businesses simply could not. As mentioned, other reality TV shows were suspended as with other forms of entertainment.

This was a period of lockdowns and no vaccine; yet production (filming) crews and construction workers, associated supply chain workers, hospitality and other allied workers were permitted to access the site. Some of these workers remained onsite and were likely subject to COVID-19 rules in place at the site. However, others such as delivery drivers would have only temporarily attended on or near the site; thereby making enforcement of onsite rules problematic for the reduction in viral transmission (consider the intense level of activity during plaster delivery at E33:47:15). The footage in that scene depicted a very busy workplace.

At the height of the first wave of the virus and in the same month Season 16 was first aired, the then Premier of Victoria said this:

> This cannot be more serious, and it's not about anything other than being… absolutely straight up: if we don't make these changes, then we're not going to get through this. *Daniel Andrews, Premier of Victoria, Australia, announcing the Stage 4 COVID-19 lockdown on August 02, 2020.* (cited in McKosker, 2021)

McKosker (2021) provides a critical account of confusion, quarantine mismanagement and constant waves of community transmissions throughout Victoria in 2020 through various stages. By the time the show was due to be aired Victoria was in a state of disaster and only essential front-line workers were not subject to harsh lockdown laws. There was no vaccine in sight (vaccines rolled out in 2021). The only strategies universally accepted were to physically distance, avoid crowds and close contact, *properly* fitted mask use when physical distancing was not possible and in poorly ventilated settings, and hand cleaning using alcohol-based products. In Victoria in 2020, specific building and construction industry were rapidly implemented to ensure minimisation of further disruption. For example, the March 2020 guideline stipulated the maximum number of personnel allowed in an area or group consistent with the Government directives. If outdoor work, workers should keep 1.5 m–2.0 m from other workers at all times. If indoor work, there should be no more than 1 worker per 4 sq m (2020: 5). This observance was also made in the context that staggered working hours had to also be considered in the Victorian Covid-19 Building Guidelines. The August iteration of that guideline revised physical distancing to least 1.5 metres should be implemented wherever possible (2020).

Yet it was obvious to the audience the construction completion time was compressed and very time-sensitive. There can be no doubt that Season 16 was a hive of activity, and permitting the completion of this undertaking for television unequivocally supports the conclusion that The Block was a serious workplace event where essential work was being performed. It was not some banal TV show.

REFERENCES

Broadcasting Services Act 1992
Broadcasting Services (Australian Content and Children's Television) Standards 2020).
Buaya, A. (2020). *It's 2020, are we still commenting on people's weight? Fans of the block are left fuming at foreman Keith Schleiger for his 'fat shaming' comments about contestant Daniel Joyce.* https://www.dailymail.co.uk/tvshowbiz/article-8759503/The-Block-fans-left-fuming-foreman-Keith-Schleigers-fat-shaming-comments.html. Accessed 31 October 2022.
Code of Practice: Managing the Risk of Psychosocial Hazards at Work (Queensland)
Collins, P. (2021). *More conflict on the block as Georgia Caceres becomes 'fed up' with foremen Keith Schleiger and Dan Reilly.* https://www.dailymail.co.uk/tvshowbiz/article-10105419/The-Block-Georgia-Caceres-fed-foremen-Keith-Dan.html
Commercial Television Industry Code of Practice.
Free Commercial Television Industry Code of Practice.
Green v Seven Network (Operations) Limited [2021] NSWPIC 75.
McCosker, L. (2021). Reflections on one of the world's harshest COVID-19 lockdowns, and on the possibility of eliminating COVID-19 in Australia. *HPHR, 29.* https://doi.org/10.54111/0001/cc5
Model *Managing psychosocial hazards at work Code of Practice*, SafeWork Australia July 2022.
Model Work Health and Safety Act 2011
Mrad, M. (2023). *The block bombshell: Producers make 'major edits' as they change show's ending... after ACMA received several complaints against*

Channel Nine's latest season. https://www.dailymail.co.uk/tvshowbiz/article-12691515/The-Block-bombshell-Producers-make-major-edits-change-shows-ending-ACMA-received-complaints-against-Channel-Nines-latest-season.html. Accessed 15 February 2024.
Occupational Health and Safety 2004.
Prince v Seven Network (Operations) Limited [2019] NSWWCC 313.
Victoria State Government. (2020). *Restrictions*. https://www.premier.vic.gov.au/sites/default/files/2021-08/20210805%20Restrictions%20Change.pdf
Work Health and Safety Regulation 2011 (Qld).

CHAPTER 3

The Block 2020 Season 16 and Its Ordinary Participants

Abstract This chapter introduces the 10 contestants of The Block within the reality TV framework setting. This chapter relies on Maslow's theoretical framework to support the observation that safety is also a motivating factor whether that be financial, psychological or physical. The show promotes the notion that shelter is essential for economic survival. This primary safety need is vital for wellbeing of the contestants. That is, the contestants are essentially aspiring to create foundations for building a better family life and the fact all the couples built five glorious homes together did represent a sense of community. This chapter considers the relevant literature concerning motivational factors for people to enter reality TV and concludes The Block's contestants possess clear reasons for entering the contest. These include primary human needs and self-actualisation which contribute to overall health and wellbeing.

Keywords Maslow · The Block contestants · Shelter · Reality TV

Irrespective of what motivates seemingly ordinary people to let themselves be captured on the reality reel, these shows enliven affective interest by the viewing audience (Kavka, 2008: 52). A significant body of research exists as to how reality TV as a genre promotes antisocial

© The Author(s), under exclusive license to Springer Nature Switzerland AG 2024
T. Cvetkovski, *Reality Television and the Art of Trivialising Work Health, Safety and Wellbeing*,
https://doi.org/10.1007/978-3-031-64098-8_3

behaviour (Hill, 2005; Holmes, 2006; Kavka, 2008) and as set out in Chapter 2, these exploitative practices have been identified by authorities (see Australian Commercial TV CoP, 2010). For example, exploitative, demeaning editing techniques, narrative exaggeration, factual distortion, conflict creation to provoke participants to react, cry, yell and generally create dramatic scenes to attract viewership have been adequately identified in the literature (Rojek, 2001).

As determined in the *Prince* case (2019), such manipulation can have lasting detrimental effects on participants' self-esteem, and this legal finding supports conclusions made in the literature that these shows can lead to personal and economic harm (Skeggs & Wood, 2012). However, The Block does not appear to seek any voyeuristic urges to explore exploitation or the creation of artificial drama during the process (compare Pinseler's (2010) examination of punitive reality TV shows). If anything, based on complaints from Block fans, the audience genuinely appears to be invested in the finished product—the house, and the creation of a tangible asset. It would be inaccurate to suggest The Block is like other reality TV where participants are predominantly placed in bizarre settings or contrived environments designed to elicit specific reactions, pushing them beyond their comfort zones and manipulating their emotions to express entertainment value (Kavka, 2012; Kilborn, 2003; Ouellette & Murray, 2009; Rojek, 2001). To that end consider Love Island, Survivor, Big Brother, Married at First Sight or Bachelor/ Bachelorette where the primary premise is on relationship development (and dysfunction).

Literature also exists on the exploitative nature of reality TV in terms of pre-existing vulnerabilities of contestants (Bignell, 2005; Skeggs & Wood, 2012). There can be no doubt casting for The Block preferred contestants pursuing the great Australian dream of home ownership. Some had personal struggles (unwell children), and others had dreams of financial security. All these relate to ordinary vicissitudes of life (Lewis, 2004). But these cannot be construed as vulnerabilities. There is nothing extraordinary about ordinary Australians seeking financial reward through a life-changing opportunity. There is a distinct purpose for entering the contest and it is accepted there is an uneven power dynamic, where producers hold significant control over editing and how identities are portrayed. In Season 16 Jimmy (H5) for example was portrayed in a very different light to Harry (H1). But despite personality profiling, what separates The Block from other reality TV is that all the couples made significant wins and realised their dreams (see Table 3.1). The show therefore is not economically exploitative per se, in that there exists a generous market exchange between those who own the means of production and capital, and those who provide their labour power. Indeed, Season 16 contestants capitalised significantly and some were extremely financially successful.

What makes *The Block* distinguishable from reality TV shows identified in the literature is that housing construction is a basic and fundamentally major yet normal undertaking that has a body of socio-economic and cultural knowledge attached to it. A house is not an artificial construct. Unlike exploitative genres such as romance or dating shows, makeovers, hidden cameras, schadenfreude-inspired law and enforcement programs and talent contests, a reality TV show premised on housing construction is a legitimate and socially acceptable business venture. In other words, The Block's producers are responsible for the construction and sale of domestic dwellings and there is nothing remarkable about this undertaking. Of course, The Block is replete with staged competitions and manufactured scenarios, competitions and games for entertainment value (Biressi & Nunn, 2005; Hill, 2005), but is argued the reason viewers watch the show is for the main objective—the build. All other reasons are secondary, and despite criticism that the show is premised on unrealistic construction timeframe expectations it cannot be denied that significant economic capital has been produced; essentially satisfying one of the most important human needs (see below).

The Block's appeal is premised on the idea that anyone, with the right work attitude, could be a participant. The following observation perhaps best summarises the motivation for applying to part of such teledrama:

> It's that time of year again when ordinary Australians quit their day jobs and take to our television screens to battle it out in the realm of reality television. The most recent trend in reality TV sees contestants trading in laptops and highlighters for hard hats & sledgehammers, all for the chance of having their living rooms remodelled, mortgages paid off, or winning that dream home. (Pro-Blog, 2014)

As Holmes explains, it is "the emphasis on the ordinariness of the contestants which contributes to the deliberate blurring between contestant and viewer and, as a result, a potential invocation of the audience's own aspirations" (2004: 156). Table 1 lists the contestants who personify the

Table 3.1 Season 16 The Block Couples[1]

House	Couple Team	Age	Origin	Relationship	Vocation
1, 1920s	Harry & Tash Pavlou	57 & 32	Melbourne, Victoria	Parent & Sibling	IT manager & Project Manager
2, 1940s	Sarah & George Bragias	27 & 32	Sydney, NSW	Married	High school teacher & Licensed electrician
3, 1930s	Jade & Daniel Joyce	34 & 35	Wandearah, SA	Married with children	Hairdresser & Farmer carpenter
4, 1910s	Luke & Jasmin Neuwen	35 & 36	Perth, WA	Married with children	Carpenter & Primary school teacher
5, 1950s	Tam & Jimmy Wilkins	31 & 33	Brisbane, Queensland	Married with child	Bar manager & Plumber

1 https://9now.nine.com.au/the-block/2020-contestants-blockheads-teams-season-16/48b9900a-fcab-4a5c-bc8d-e64fb85be17.

spectacle of the hardworking but ordinary individual capable of achieving success in the execution of an undertaking (Dyer, 1998; Ritchie, 2000; Rojek, 2001).

The Block, created and produced by Cavalier Television Pty Ltd, is Australia's most popular Australian reality TV show and is also syndicated globally (OzTAM, 2023; Simpson, 2004). For this study, the 50 episodes aired had Australian viewership per episode which ranged from 0.65 to 1.29 million across five major cities (OzTAM, 2023). Free-to-air on the Nine Network service, the season premiered on 23 August 2020 and comprised the long-serving host and former builder Scott Cam and co-host Shelley Craft, site forepersons (managers/supervisors) and qualified builders Keith Schleiger and Dan Reilly, and room reveal judges Neale Whitaker, Shaynna Blaze and Darren Palmer. The format of the show is produced in a popular reality TV style where couple participants enter a contest to renovate, restore and otherwise build a residential dwelling with the ultimate goal of auctioning it to the highest bidder. The premise for the 2020 season was a vacant block of land in Brighton, Australia in which five dilapidated or derelict 1910s–1950s period houses were renovated, extended and otherwise converted into multi-million dollar prestige properties.

House team couples were required to be available for a 10–12 week period in 2020. After the major COVID-19 disruption in March 2020, couples left the worksite due to lockdown and border closures. Full production resumed in May 2020. The nature of services was exclusive in that no outside work was permitted during the filming period and previous home renovation experience was not essential but regarded as an asset according to marketing material (The Block, 2020). Participants were paid nominal weekly fees. Even as the works were disrupted by the first Covid Lockdown period, they were compensated for time lost (Courier Mail, 2020).

The teams were given weekly budgets, and with the assistance of tradespersons were responsible for the renovation and extension of various rooms. Remuneration for works performed, provision of tools and materials to perform work, use of work cars to collect supplies, uniforms and PPE were supplied by the producers who controlled the work undertaking. Construction included not only the dwelling but also the front garden, façade, studio, garage backyard and pool. The teams were responsible for project managing the works as directed by the production team (bedrooms, kitchen, bathroom and so on). At the end of each task, the judges assessed the project and awarded points. The projects were funded by the production company, points were aggregated, and the highest-scoring couple controlled the auction order. The 2020 season finale ended with an auction day spectacle in late November 2020. Not only did Tam and Jimmy (Couple 5, H5)) accrue the most points and control the order of the auction, but they earned $966,000 in profit at auction in addition to $100,000 in prize money.[2]

The Block allows audiences to connect with the characters. This sense of authenticity is further reinforced by the aspiration of homeownership, which in the hierarchy of needs context, is fundamental to wellbeing according to the Australian government (AIHW, 2023). The show has become a powerful combination of emotive audience captivation, drama associated with renovation and satisfaction of seeing a dream home come to life. Viewers may live vicariously through the homeowners but feel a strong connectedness with real experience or aspiration to transform outdated or dilapidated spaces into stunning living areas. The show offers design ideas and brand inspiration by showcasing diverse styles, innovative solutions for common problems, and the latest trends in home improvement (refer to the Block website for evidence of this). Despite fan commentary about the timeframes, the contestants faced relatable challenges, such as tight budgets, conflicting design preferences, or unexpected obstacles during the renovation process. The show, it is argued does create a relatable connection with the audience, and it is only natural house favourites would be formed based on the aesthetics of the project. But relevantly, viewers gain valuable insights from experienced designers, contractors, and other professionals involved in the renovation process. The power of The Block is that it is educative, and what it portrays to the audience about housing is appealing.

---

[2] Couple 2 received $605,002, followed by Couple 1 ($605,000), then Couple 4 ($506,000) and Couple 3 ($460,000).

Food (McDonalds), Clothing (Bisley Workwear) and Shelter (Building a Home): *What's Maslow's Hierarchy of Needs Got to Do with the Block?*

It is accepted that the show attempts to blend creativity, inspiration, entertainment and of course marketing and commodification. This subtitle above is a reference to the significant representation of commercial food and beverage sponsorship (McDonalds) and clothing (Bisley) depicted on the show. However, the focus here is squarely on shelter as a primary need which is at the primary level in the hierarchy of needs as theorised by Abraham Maslow (1943). This need can only be satisfied if an individual has sufficient financial capacity to purchase items that fulfil this need. It cannot be construed as anything but a need to be both financially secure and physically and mentally safe.

The point of difference with this form of reality TV is that in light of this Maslovian framework, it also appeals to DIY enthusiast renovators, designers and people who simply enjoy watching the transformation of homes and who aspire to renovate their dream home one day. The appeal is not voyeuristic per se. These shows are educative; not in the pedagogical sense, but there is an argument to suggest The Block is andragogic in its practical presentation of work to the viewing audience. That is the audience might accept that the show is a form of entertainment as a means of popular culture, but the reality is that at auction time, the ends are centred around maximising profit from the sale of a house at market value. How is this aspiration any different from the viewing audience striving to sell their own property to the highest bidder? The Block is significantly influential because its focus is on a most fundamental and primary hierarchal need—shelter.

Following Maslow's basic hierarchy of needs, shelter is one of the most basic levels of needs inclusive of safety. Higher order ideals such as belonging, creativity, community participation and other popular socio-cultural ideals such as love, identity, achievement, self-esteem and self-actualisation are subordinated by this primary need (Dutil, 2022). These other Maslovian ideals may also be essential ingredients for reality TV, but when a basic need such as shelter is added to a format the program becomes more serious because the participants are striving to create a future for their families. Evidence for this observation is readily provided from the interviews of the participants. For example, Jimmy and

Tam, The Block season's winners (and favourites) were very clear about their motivation for being on the show. Jimmy explained:

> *Currently renting and working endless hours, the pair hope to use their winnings to buy a home of their own. We are doing this for Frankie. We want to try and win to set our family up. We had all quit our jobs and put our life on hold. Having to come home to such an unstable economic climate, you couldn't go and get a new job and say, "I might have to leave if I get a call from The Block.* (Walters, 2020)

Jimmy also explained how the show's producers arranged for them to be paid once they returned (Walters, 2020). This couple's dream was realised when as result of the profit from the sale of H5, Jimmy and Tam purchased their "first family home" (Nine Now, 2021). These remarks suggest the young family, unsurprisingly, sought security and stability in their lives, and by providing a home, Jimmy was addressing safety and protection needs. Furthermore, owning a home fosters a sense of predictability and control, reducing anxiety and fear associated with uncertainty Maslow, 1943).

On the one hand, critics may accuse The Block of promoting consumerism as homeowners aspire to prioritise aesthetics and resale through profit value over functionality and sustainability. This is a valid argument given the pivotal role the judges play and the emphasis on high-end finishes and on-trend designs which contribute to a culture of excess, rather than promoting responsible and sustainable home improvement practices. However, the show does also support eco-friendly design and practice. It was reported for the 2022 season the project was completely "off-grid and more ambitiously sustainable than anything we've seen on the show before" (Hone, 2022). In any event, the show promotes the primary urge to ensure stability and security through homeownership first followed by aspirational desires.

Maslow's theoretical framework is important because it supports the observation that safety is also a motivating factor whether that be financial, psychological or physical (Wilkins, 2011). The show promotes the fact that shelter is essential for economic survival. Clearly food, water, and air are obviously vital, but having a safe place (consider Harry (H5) the protective father's motives or any of the couples for that matter) and future home security is vital for protection from real world danger such as not affording a home. These primary safety needs are vital for wellbeing. In short increasing capacity to satisfy these basic needs improves health and safety and wellbeing (Trigg, 2004) for the contestants. That is, they are essentially aspiring to create foundations for building a better family life, and the fact all the couples are building five glorious homes together, the show does represent a sense of community. This primary desire is a clear motivating factor for competing on this show. There are less clear factors as to why people would enter several other reality TV genres, but The Block is grounded in a pivotal need for not only survival but self-actualisation thereby contributing to overall health and wellbeing (Maslow, 1943).[3]

Reality TV Manipulation and Audience Interaction and Concerns

The Block is one of the most popular reality shows in Australia and its longevity is enduring proof that its appeal is rooted in the audience's primary interest around the need for shelter. However, this observation is not without its critics concerning how the show portrays housing projects. *Grand Designs Australia* host Peter Maddison was very scathing when he said, "I hate *The Block*, it's absolute bloody nonsense…it should be banned from television because it leaves people with the false aspirations that they can become – in inverted commas – a project manager or a builder or a designer. It's a joke…It's a very bad example of the reality of building, the responsibilities around that and the difficulty of it all" (in Talbot, 2023).

The concerns ventilated by Maddison, intersect to some extent with issues raised in this research given the serious nature of the undertaking. An examination of social media reveals not only is the show influential in terms of design aesthetics, but online comments address some concerns around WHSW. These audience views are supported by media reports concerning injuries and treatment of contestants. Consider the *Builder's Wife (Nicole)* website and corresponding blog. In two threads entitled *Let's Talk The Block And Why I Don't Watch* (commenced 2017) and *Why Builders Hate The Block* (commenced 2016) which have attracted

---

[3] Refer to T. Cvetkovski (2015) for an examination of reality TV contestant legitimacy and authenticity.

nearly 10,000 views and 25 comments, several comments were about the "optics" of the show concerning WHSW. Some of the comments from builders include:

- *As a carpenter/builder myself it also frustrates me watching the trades rush and struggle...I actually have first hand experience with the mess on The Block...never have I seen workmanship this appalling...dangerous wiring and electrical which was far from Australian standards, structural supports missing...* (Zachary Dawson, 2019);
- *Too much unneeded pressure and stress in that show* (Grace, 2016);
- *I often wonder about the hours through the night to get the job done* (Clare, 2016);
- *It is really quite horrifying that this can happen. I mean if we were to create such a mess the governing bodies would be there to sort it out ASAP* (Nicole, 2019).

The consistent theme to emerge in the public domain is that the show does place unrealistic expectations where "everyone is exhausted and stressed" (Johnson, 2022). The point of these observations is The Block does attract publicity which intersects with WHSW issues, and safety is a primary motivating human factor. As the nature of the work is serious in every respect, it is for this reason that the audience can relate to activities being undertaken and the responses aired publicly are understandable. To scrutinise remarks made by participant workers around lack of sleep and limited resources to complete stages of work are matters which seem to motivate the audience to raise concerns. Pursuant to the *Model Code of Practice on Managing Psychosocial Codes of Practices* these matters could be classified as fatigue, high job demands, low job control, unrealistic job expectations or inadequate job support. It is argued these experiences potentially compromise participants' agency which could lead to feelings of anxiety or psychological distress.

REFERENCES

AIHW. (2023). *Home ownership and housing tenure*. https://www.aihw.gov.au/reports/australias-welfare/home-ownership-and-housing-tenure

Australian Commercial TV CoP. (2010). *Commercial television industry code of practice (January 2010-incorporating amendments to July 2013)*. Australian Communications and Media Authority.

Bignell, J. (2005). *Big Brother: Reality TV in the twenty-first century*. Palgrave Macmillan.

Biressi, A., & Nunn, H. (2005). *Reality TV: Realism and revelation* Wallflower Press.

Courier Mail. (2020). *The block 2020: Contestants paid wage during COVID-19*. https://www.couriermail.com.au›confidential›news-story. Accessed 22 April 2021.

Dutil, P. (2022). What do people want from politics? rediscovering and repurposing the "Maslow Hierarchy" to teach political needs. *Journal of Political Science Education, 18*(1), 138–149. https://doi.org/10.1080/15512169.2021.1987259

Dyer, R. (1998). *Stars*. BFI Publishing.

Hill, A. (2005). *Reality TV: Audiences and popular factual television*. Routledge.

Holmes, S. (2004). Reality goes pop! Reality TV, popular music, and narratives of stardom in *Pop Idol*. *Television & New Media, 5*(2), 147–172.

Holmes, S. (2006). When will i be famous?. In D Escofferry (Ed.), *How real is reality TV?* McFarland.

Johnson, K. (2022). *Channel Nine deny claims conditions on The Block are 'brutal' with minimal food and no access to Uber Eats: 'Everyone knows the show is tough'*. https://www.dailymail.co.uk/tvshowbiz/article-10862449/Channel-Nine-deny-claims-conditions-Block-inhumane-brutal.html

Kavka, M. (2008). *Reality television, affect and intimacy*. Palgrave Macmillan.

Kavka, M. (2012). *Reality TV*. Edinburgh University Press.

Kilborn, R. (2003). *Staging the real: Factual programming in the age of Big Brother*. Manchester University Press.

Lewis, J. (2004). The meaning of real life. In S Murray & L. Ouellette (Eds.), *Reality TV: Remaking television culture*. New York University Press.

Maslow, A. H. (1943). A theory of human motivation. *Psychological Review, 50*, 370–396.

Nine Network. (2020). https://9now.nine.com.au/the-block/2020-contestants-blockheads-teams-season-16/48b9900a-fcab-4a5c-bc8d-e64ffb85be17

Nine Now. (2021). The Block https://9now.nine.com.au/the-block/jimmy-tam-2020-winners-buy-first-family-house/07459e7e-f9a0-4d58-b4f4-57c3d8f76185

Ouellette, L., & Murray, S. (2009). Introduction. In S. Murray & L. Ouellette (Eds.), *Reality TV: Remaking television culture*. New York University Press.

Offe, C. (1985). *Disorganized capitalism*. Polity.
OzTam. (2023). https://oztam.com.au/latestavailablereports.aspx. Accessed 31 January 2023.
Pinseler, J. (2010). Punitive Reality TV: Televising punishment and the production of law and order. In S. Van Bauwel & N. Carpenter (Eds.), *Trans-reality television: The transgression of reality, genre, politics, and audience* (pp. 125–148). Lexington Books.
Prince v Seven Network (Operations) Limited [2019] NSWWCC 313.
Pro-Blog. (2014). *Growing popularity of DIY causes a rise in accidental injuries*. https://prochoicesafetygear.com/ppe/blog/ohs/growing-popularity-of-diy-causes-a-rise-in-accidental-injuries/
Ritchie, J. (2000). *Big Brother: The official unseen story*. Channel Four Books.
Rojek, C. (2001). *Celebrity*. Reaktion Books.
Simpson, T. (2004). *The block: Open for inspection*. ACP Pub.
Skeggs, B., & Wood, H. (2012). *Reacting to reality television: Performance, audience, value*. Routledge.
Talbot, L. (2023). *Controversy swamps The Block amid housing crisis*. https://www.thenewdaily.com.au/entertainment/2023/03/29/the-block-controversy-grand-designs
The Builder's Wife Blog. (2019). *Why builders hate the block—the builder's wife. (thebuilderswife.com.au)*
Wilkins, J. (2011). Construction workers' perceptions of health and safety training programmes. *Construction Management and Economics, 29*(10), 1017–1026. https://doi.org/10.1080/01446193.2011.633538

CHAPTER 4

Theoretical Underpinnings for the Data

Abstract Two theoretical underpinnings which guide this research are explained in this chapter. The first is the cultural theory of risk perception. This theory is applied to The Block because wider moral questions are posed about categorising workplace practices within a social discourse. The second theoretical underpinning guiding this study is trivialisation as a mode of dissonance. The result of this dissonance is to reduce the activities to trivialisation because they are not seen as risky or unacceptable actions (Simon et al., Journal of Personality and Social Psychology 68: 247, 1995). These theories assist in explaining why the individual on The Block potentially reduced the importance of certain elements of WHSW.

Keywords Cognitive bias · Cultural theory · Dissonance risk perception · Trivialisation

Cultural Risk Theory/Cultural Theory of Risk[1]

Of theoretical significance to this study is how behaviours are shaped through social construction of risk (von Scheve & Lange, 2023). In *Risk and Culture* (1982), Douglas and Wildavsky introduced cultural theory (CT) to risk analysis (RA). Risk perception attitudes inform RA and a central argument of Douglas and Wildavsky (1982) is that cultural biases determine which hazards pose high or low risk. Judgements about what is or is not dangerous or harmful is a social construct and as Tansey and O'Riordan contend, individuals do not assess risks independently of social context (1999: 71). For example, the law may prescribe what is a high-risk activity (work at height or asbestos management). Attitudes and beliefs of individuals about risk analysis are influenced by value systems belonging to specific groups who form bonded cultural relationships (Tansey and O'Riordan, 1999 p. 71). For example, specific legal guidance is provided to member groups of society who are involved in serious or high-risk work-related events, incidents or accidents including work at height or exposure to silica dust. Therefore in the absence of prescription, "individuals choose what to fear" and are motivated by decisions determined in that social setting (Wildavsky & Dake, 1990: 43). It is argued risks are socially created to serve the social relations of those perceiving and analysing them (Bourdieu, 1977) and data obtained from the reality TV series The Block empirically validates this cultural bias argument in which relations are prescribed.

Cultural Risk Theory (CRT) is utilised in this undertaking because it offers sociological insights into how cultural factors at work intersect with risk perception, communication, and management in the workplace. This theoretical framework is important for understanding that risk perceptions are not solely determined by objective measures of danger but are deeply influenced by cultural norms, attitudes values, and symbolic meanings concerning both the likelihood and severity of potential harm (Jacoby, 2006; Schwartz, 1992). Perception of risk is ultimately a psychosocial process. Outlooks based on social solidarities about how risk is communicated imply how risk is collectively viewed as a cultural process. As such, CRT theory focuses on these shared values which are formed by people in groups through their interactions in the social world (Gross & Rayner, 1985).

---

[1] Used interchangeably with Cultural Theory of Risk.

How individuals' interpretations of risk are determined is based on the environment. At the core of CRT is the notion that individuals' perceptions of risk and shapes their attitudes towards various hazards are prioritised; thereby influencing their risk assessments and responses (Feldman, 2003). The law as the supreme instrument of governance and control deems reckless conduct and industrial manslaughter to be the most dangerous of all WHSW considerations. For example, a worker working at a height of six metres on the edge of a roof with no edge protection highly increases the likelihood of serious injury or death from a fall at height. In this scenario, an employer not providing a physical barrier would be considered unacceptable in any given cultural context, and all solidarity and trust of the collective (society) would erode if workers' lives were put in serious danger (Durkheim, 1893). This is why the law prescribes work at height activity as high risk (see for example the *Model Work Health and Safety Regulation*). Alternatively, the risk of slipping arising from leads strewn on the work floor would be starkly contrasted to working at height without fall arrest protection because on any objective assessment, the likelihood of serious harm would be so low that there would be little or no regard to the consequences of not complying by having a messy work floor. Accordingly, cultural biases may amplify or attenuate perceived risks, impacting individuals' willingness to engage in risk-taking behaviour or adopt precautionary measures. The level of solidarity for say PPE adherence would be lower because there would exist a tendency for individuals to interpret risk through the lens of their cultural worldview, leading to cognitive biases and distortions in risk perception.

The theory is applicable to the show because the individuals depicted created bonds (solidarity), and looked for information and communication about risks in a collective manner. The cultural theory of risk perception is applied to The Block because wider moral questions are posed about categorising workplace practices within a social discourse. To the individual, what is the value of PPE or what does it matter if signage is ignored; especially as administrative control is so low on the order of hierarchy of control and elimination? What norms have materially transgressed by social groups to warrant a reduction in risky behaviour or poor cultural practices at work simply because jokes are made in poor taste, archaic, gendered language is used, or alcohol is permitted on a construction site? It is contended risks are socially created to serve the social relations of those perceiving and analysing them. In this context, CT is useful in providing a critical framework for analysis of how hazards are interpreted, identified and assessed, and what normative value is placed on whether there is any likelihood of risk attached to a hazard (Douglas, 1992). As a form of collective conscience, CT of risk perception is applied to the subsequent influence of specific cultural biases in this reality show because CT assists in understanding how specific social groups interact at workplaces in order to determine their values and outlooks about conventional and emerging risks (Douglas, 1992).

Applying Trivialisation Dissonance to Cultural Theory of Risk

Drawing on an understanding of cultural bias, values placed at the lower end of any risk perception evaluation are akin to ranking the likelihood of harm at the bottom of any risk assessment. The attitude expected from the group of participants by placing a low value on any event is indicative of a trivial response to a particular hazard in that cultural setting. In other words, the generation of concern might be low but the level of casualisation or indifference from those holding certain cultural biases might be high.

As defined in Chapter 1, trivialisation occurs when individuals downplay the significance of certain behaviours or actions because they perceive them to be less in importance of value. In the workplace. The lower the value the more trivial the outlook toward risk (Simon et al., 1995). Risk trivialisation dissonance arises when individuals engage in behaviours that contradict societal values by diminishing the importance of specific actions because of a perceived likelihood that the risk is insignificant or does not warrant attention. This approach can manifest in various ways, often subtly and unconsciously. For example, someone who genuinely values safety might also downplay the significance of sign observance or ignore clutter at the site. The fact The Block was fast-paced and competitive in nature provides a good case study for workplaces that might attract risk trivialisation and the dissonance that flows from this. Similarly, applying CRT to the understanding risk trivialisation, accepting or tolerating the presence of alcohol onsite might be justified on the grounds that it is not actually being consumed when work is being conducted. Furthermore, accepting pressure to meet unrealistic deadlines and deliver work at any cost might be justified on the ground that everyone else is going through the same stress (e.g. see Hell Week in E37). Participants convince themselves this is the status quo or that The Block is a tough work environment. The risk of fatigue, exhaustion or burnout is downplayed or presented in a stoic manner because of the cultural bias that exists about the potential for this psychosocial hazard (Maslach & Leiter, 2016). The risk with trivialisation is that it does leave people disengaged from their principles to justify their actions. This can further exacerbate negative behaviour and create a culture of acceptance of suboptimal attitudes about WHSW thereby challenging personal integrity and eroding trust within teams (Breuer et al., 2020).

As risk trivialisation is the process of downplaying the seriousness or significance of a potential danger it is a cognitive bias where individuals or groups minimise the likelihood or severity of a negative outcome associated with a particular action or situation (Aven, 2013). This can lead to increased risk-taking behaviour and a neglect of necessary safety precautions. By downplaying the severity, individuals convince themselves that the potential consequences of a risky action are minor or inconsequential, and are less likely to take steps to mitigate them. People might therefore underestimate the probability of a negative outcome occurring, leading them to believe they are safe even when engaging in risky behaviour. Individuals might also justify their risky actions by observing others engaging in similar behaviour without negative consequences. This creates a sense of normalcy and reduces their perceived risk. For example, an employee might bypass safety measures like wearing PPE because they find it uncomfortable or inconvenient. Employees might rush through tasks, neglecting important safety checks to meet tight deadlines. The consequence of risk trivialisation is that it can create a culture where safety becomes less prioritised leading to a dilution of the value of lower order or low-risk awareness among employees and thereby causing dissonance among workers.

Risk trivialisation is applied to determine the extent of downplaying or underestimating the severity or likelihood of potential dangers or negative outcomes associated with a particular action or situation. This cognitive bias occurs when individuals or groups minimise the significance of risks, in a given cultural setting and that bias results in increased risk-taking behaviour or a neglect of necessary safety precautions. The show presents this conduct as a form of dissonance which trivialises the importance of HSW cognitions concerned with specific activities or behaviours.

The type of cultural system (Parsons, 1951) is reflected in The Block as a set of social actions (Bourdieu, 1984) which comprise ideas and beliefs, symbols and values internalised by the individual actors (Mulkay, 1971) and are reduced to lower importance; namely trivialisation. Cultural theory supports the argument certain perceived risks are endured in this habitus as shared experiences; or as solidarities of outlook (Bourdieu, 1990). The acceptance or normalisation of these behaviours exposes a certain collective tolerance and subsequent trivialisation of some risks as unimportant, low order or "acceptable risks" (Douglas, 1992). Cultural values, beliefs, and social structures inform evaluation of risk because cultural biases influence what is perceived as dangerous and what is not (Douglas & Wildavsky, 1982). In this tele-sphere, it seems the show's participants are engaging in activities that are an authentic representation of a workplace habitus (Bourdieu & Passeron, 1977) that is in support of trivialisation as a common mode of dissonance. The regularity of several identifiable HSW events suggests likelihood of risk was perceived so low that these behaviours were normalised through trivialisation.

REFERENCES

Aven, T. (2013). On how to deal with deep uncertainties in a risk assessment and management context. *Risk Analysis, 33*(12), 2082–2091. https://doi.org/10.1111/risa.12067

Bourdieu, P. (1977). *Outline of a theory of practice*. Cambridge University Press.

Bourdieu, P. (1984). *Distinction: A social critique of the judgement of taste*. Harvard University Press.

Bourdieu, P. (1990). Structures, habitus, practices, in the logic of practice. *Polity*, 52–65.

Bourdieu, P., & Passeron, J. (1977). *Reproduction in education society and culture*. Sage.

Breuer, C., Hüffmeier, J., Hibben, F., & Hertel, G. (2020). Trust in teams: A taxonomy of perceived trustworthiness factors and risk-taking behaviors in face-to-face and virtual teams. *Human Relations, 73*(1), 3–34. https://doi.org/10.1177/0018726718818721

Douglas, M., & Wildavsky, A. (1982). *Risk and culture: An essay on the selection of technological and environmental dangers*. University of California Press.

Douglas, P. M. (1992). *Risk and blame: Essays in cultural theory*. Routledge.

Durkheim, E. (1960 [1893]). *The division of labor in society* (G. Simpson, Trans.). Free Press of Glencoe.

Feldman, S. (2003). Values, ideology, and the structure of political attitudes. In D. O. Sears, L. Huddy, & R. Jervis (Eds.), *Oxford handbook of political psychology* (pp. 477–508). Oxford University Press.

Festinger, L. (1957). A *theory of cognitive dissonance*. Row, Peterson.

Gross, J. L., & Rayner, S. (1985). *Measuring culture*. Columbia University Press.
Jacoby, W. (2006). Value choices and American public opinion. *American Journal of Political Science, 50*(3), 706–723.
Maslach, C., & Leiter, M. P. (2016). Understanding the burnout experience: Recent research and its implications for psychiatry. *World Psychiatry, 15*(2), 103–111. https://doi.org/10.1002/wps.20311.PMID:27265691;PMCID:PMC4911781
Mulkay, M. (1971). *Functionalism, exchange and the theoretical strategy*. Routledge & Kegan Paul.
Parsons, T. (1951). *The social system*. Free Press.
Schwartz, S. (1992). Universals in the content and structure of values: Theoretical advances and empirical tests in 20 countries. *Advances in Experimental Social Psychology, 25*, 1–65.
Simon, L., Greenberg, J., & Brehm, J. (1995). Trivialization: The forgotten mode of dissonance reduction. *Journal of Personality and Social Psychology, 68*(2), 247. https://doi.org/10.1037/0022-3514.68.2.247
Tansey, J., & O'riordan, T. (1999). Cultural theory and risk: A review. *Health, Risk & Society, 1*(1), 71–90. https://doi.org/10.1080/13698579908407008
von Scheve, C., & Lange, M. (2023). Risk entanglement and the social relationality of risk. *Humanities and Social Sciences Communications, 10*, 170. https://doi.org/10.1057/s41599-023-01668-0
Wildavsky, A., & Dake, K. (1990). Theories of risk perception: Who fears what and why? *Daedalus, 119*(4), 41–60.

CHAPTER 5

Method and Measurement

Abstract This chapter sets out the methods and measurement adopted in the study. The design of the research was exploratory and was used to examine values about certain workplace activities commonly clustered or perceived to be ranked at the lower end of risk and therefore less dangerous or harmful (if at all). An observational design was applied since the purpose was to attempt to detect and code patterns of activities, conduct and behaviours by repeatedly watching the entire season. The intention was to identify potential activities, analyse the content and evaluate specific themes particularised in six broad typologies. Adopting this observational approach, Season 16 (2020) ($n = 50$ episodes) was critically reviewed on three separate occasions to assess the level of trivialisation of identifiable hazards and controls. The following propositions were tested: (1) onsite skylarking, inattention and lax PPE usage were tolerated or downplayed in certain instances; (2) safety signage compliance was inconsistent throughout the season; (3) site untidiness and occasional hygiene issues were observed; (4) onsite consumption and promotion of alcohol appeared to be normalised; (5) antiquated gendered language or stereotyping was used; and (6) potential exposure to various psychosocial hazards was accepted or inadequately addressed on occasion. A cultural theory of risk perception was applied to events or scenes to identify specific and repeated instances of trivialisation dissonance relating to the above typologies.

© The Author(s), under exclusive license to Springer Nature Switzerland AG 2024
T. Cvetkovski, *Reality Television and the Art of Trivialising Work Health, Safety and Wellbeing*,
https://doi.org/10.1007/978-3-031-64098-8_5

Keywords Method · Measurement · Research design · Observational study · Code sheet

Drawing on cultural theory of risk perception within The Block's social structures, two sets of WHSW risk typologies were designed for observation. The first category contains clusters of tangible low order hazards that were visible or clear enough to be identified. The second category presents intangible hazards that concern language and conduct which were psychosocial in nature. For the first set, the following propositions were tested:

1. Onsite skylarking, inattention and lax PPE usage or application appeared to be tolerated or downplayed in certain instances at the workplace;
2. Site safety signage observance was inconsistent;
3. Site untidiness (mess, clutter, debris) and occasional hygiene hazards were observed as not being adequately monitored.

The second set of propositions tested were:

4. Consumption and promotion of alcohol at work appeared to be tolerated or permitted and subsequently normalised;
5. Antiquated/Archaic gendered language or stereotyping was used on the show;
6. Potential exposure to various psychosocial hazards at the workplace was observed as being accepted or inadequately addressed.

METHODOLOGICAL APPROACH

Adopting an observational approach (Krippendorff, 2018), the frequency of occurrence of specific WHSW themes contained within $n = 48$ episodes was analysed and evaluated (Episodes 49–50 were not analysed). To achieve an optimal coding process, the season was critically watched by the author when it was first televised on the Nine Network in 2020 (23 August–22 November 2020). During this phase, the show was watched holistically without coding. Each episode of the entire season was then watched and reviewed via Nine's streaming service in 2021 from September to December (second phase) and again from December 2022 to April 2023 (third phase). The flexibility of this catch-up service enabled the coder to repeatedly review segments of the episodes for coding proficiency. The purpose of reviewing twice in the subsequent phases was first to corroborate the initial observations, and secondly to a provide a more granular set of observational data. This was particularly important when scenes were short or clarification about an event demanded repeated context evaluation. The approach to the data facilitated micro-analysis of behaviors and interaction patterns to develop in-depth consideration of what was being depicted (Paterson et al., 2003). This was readily achieved because of the availability of the streaming service.

The approach to content analysis was a mixed method to assess the extent to which the activities were trivialised. A coding schedule and corresponding Excel worksheet were created to record events as they were depicted.[1] All footage excluding advertising breaks was viewed and semi-quantitatively coded into the six thematic typologies mentioned above (See Figures for total number of events).

The codebook was refined to capture incidents as scenarios or vignettes from the episodes in the form of clusters of comparable behaviours, actions or attitudes. Each event was recorded as a scene and time-coded as it was depicted or arose in the show. Despite 50 episodes in the season, the coding process was applied to Episodes 1–48 because the final two episodes exclusively concerned marketing and auctioning of the newly constructed residential dwellings. That is, no construction work was performed. The length of each episode analysed ranged from 46–86 minutes. Figures 6.1 and 6.3 record the rate of observations and 6.2 and 6.4 provide an average of events per episode from the date collected and represented in the tables. Tables 6.1 and 6.2 present the observation chronological order as follows:

- Time Stamp—00:00 = minute:second (when scene/event appeared in episode)
- H denotes house number
- Code Book created from Nine Network Streaming Service 9 Now (https://www.9now.com.au/the-block/season-16)

---

[1] The data were converted in Tables 6.1 and 6.2 respectively in Chapter 6.

- Approximate Time stamp excludes advertisements.

As the figures demonstrate, quantifying content reduces the research to ascertain the rate at which events are sustained and repeated. This may assist in determining whether conduct is systemic or not. However, some events were examined in greater detail by way of qualitative content analysis in the form of case studies as drawn from the events recorded under the typologies. This approach assisted in contextualising the nature of specific acts worthy of greater analysis. For example, qualitative analysis assisted in contextualising psychosocial events such as body shaming and making remarks about laziness or aggression at the workplace. Where presented, these qualitative data were presented as scenes or vignettes where the extracted dialogue from the relevant scene was transcribed, and time stamped. It is accepted that a limitation to this approach is that qualitative analysis of events and the context in which the events occurred is an inductive process enabling the researcher to examine the subjective interpretation of the underlying meaning of the issues identified (Krippendorff, 2018).

Research Design Justification

As set out at the outset, the design of the research was to identify the potential for risk trivialisation. The logged occurrences and subsequent discussions indicated the possibility of such activity. Another researcher may have found more events or less, but the purpose of providing a number for the discussion was to demonstrate an atmosphere of risk trivialisation did exist on the show. This approach allowed for greater flexibility when exploring specific incidents and permitted a deeper understanding of some of the scenes which seemed conflicting when considering the importance of continuous improvement in WHSW.

This methodological approach allowed for in-depth narrative exploration (qualitative) which was supported by clusters of comparable events (quantitative) to indicate that cultural bias towards risk trivialisation was consistent across the entire season (see Tariq & Woodman, 2013).[2] This mixed methods research is experimentally *conjunctive* in that it seeks to investigate causal relationships (Howe, 2012) through these two

---

[2] These authors provide a helpful analysis of the use of this mixed methods approach.

distinct but interconnected approaches. These methods are integrated through the application of case law and statutory instruments for triangulation Denzin (1978). Doctrinal developments bring objectivity to the different methods which explore the same research questions to provide a substantiated causal explanation.

Using CRT to analyse the data allowed for linkages in the power dynamics of the participants, the types of social structures, and overall environment that shaped risk perception. The mixed methods strategy supports the cultural theory framework because the cultural bias depicted on The Block is an ideological reflection of the weight attached to certain workplace behaviours. Values are "the criteria people use to select and justify actions to evaluate people (including the self) and events" (Schwartz, 1992: 1) and create the parameters for what is deemed acceptable and unacceptable at a workplace. The Block demonstrates to the audience the low value placed on the identified events (Feldman, 2003: 479), and whether these issues are important (Schwartz, 1992: 4) in terms of value structures (Jacoby, 2006: 707).

The two-tiered approach to content analysis of The Block offered valuable insights into cultural, social and psychological dimensions of this popular media genre. It allowed for an examination of the construction of the reality of behaviours that are mirrored in the world of work, representation of identities and relationships formed by ordinary working individuals. The approach has provided a framework for consideration of broader implications for the management of unresolved HSW issues at work where cognitive dissonance through trivialisation may reduce the value of certain activities and behaviours.

Rationale for the Approach to the Coding

The limitations of the method and measurement were explained in Chapter 1. But reflecting on Singh's (2012) comments in Chapter 1, the expression of interest by the former member of parliament about DIY is of significance to the design of this research. Many viewers would be aspiring renovators and DIY weekend renovators with varying degrees of skill, competence and ability. The work being depicted does resonate with work being performed in a domestic setting.

By way of illustration, the viewer may ask, legitimately about placement or use of various items of plant that are clearly potentially dangerous if used incorrectly. Table 6.1 for example contains observational coding data and lists a few instances where a Jetfire LPG electric gas heater was utilised. The instruction manual for this item of plant expressly states at p. 2:

> *Jetfire Heaters are specifically designed to solve all problems relating to heating drying and desiccating in commercial and industrial applications. Some examples of applications are in warehouse and factory heating, animal husbandry and greenhouse applications.* (Spitfire 2024)

From a system of work design perspective, the viewer is entitled to query the following points before embarking on acquiring one of these items as clearly expressed in the instructions:

- As the unit expels fumes which contain carbon monoxide, how can it be ensured the unit is operated in an area where permanent ventilation to the outside atmosphere is provided? According to the manual, **Mandatory minimum room size: 350 Meters Squared (M3)** emphasis added
- The heater must be installed with a minimum distance from surrounding walls and/or ceiling of 2 m.
- Inadequate extension cords can be dangerous. If an extension cord is used, it must be suitable for outdoor use and the connection must be kept dry and off ground. Loose extension cords and power cables provide a potential trip hazard, especially when they cross pathways. Take safety measures like placing traffic cones along the cord or tape the cord to the floor with duct tape.
- An external guard should be place 1 m away from the heater outlet to prevent the approach of combustible material (Industry Update, 2024, Spitfire, 2024).

Similarly, the coding for the intangible data in Table 3 invites the reader to reflect on the cultural environment created in this workplace, and whether some of the events should be tolerated in any setting. These reflections are important because post-Covid lockdowns, workers in recent years have become increasingly apprised of the risks and hazards associated with psychosocial harm, appropriate communications (Saladino et al., 2020) and health risks associated with alcohol consumption (Ramalho, 2020). As the show provides a fertile environment in which to explore these typologies at length, coding the events as they occurred was justified in order to set the scene for the extrapolation of specific scenes.

References

Denzin, N. K. (1978). *The research act: A theoretical introduction to sociological methods*. McGraw-Hill.

Feldman, S. (2003). Values, ideology, and the structure of political attitudes. In D. O. Sears, L. Huddy, & R. Jervis (Eds.), *Oxford handbook of political psychology* (pp. 477–508). Oxford University Press.

Howe, K. R. (2012). Mixed methods, triangulation, and causal explanation. *Journal of Mixed Methods Research, 6*(2), 89–96. https://doi.org/10.1177/1558689812437187

Jacoby, W. (2006). Value choices and American public opinion. *American Journal of Political Science, 50*(3), 706–723.

Krippendorff, K. (2018). *Content analysis: An introduction to its methodology*. Sage.

Paterson, B. L., Bottorff, J. L., & Hewat, R. (2003). Blending observational methods: Possibilities, strategies, and challenges. *International Journal of Qualitative Methods, 2*(1), 29–38. https://doi.org/10.1177/160940690300200103

Ramalho, R. (2020). Alcohol consumption and alcohol-related problems during the COVID-19 pandemic: A narrative review. *Australasian Psychiatry, 28*(5), 524–526. https://doi.org/10.1177/1039856220943024

Saladino, V., Algeri, D., & Auriemma, V. (2020). The psychological and social impact of Covid-19: New perspectives of well-being. *Frontiers in Psychology, 11*, 577684. https://doi.org/10.3389/fpsyg.2020.577684

Schwartz, S. (1992). Universals in the content and structure of values: Theoretical advances and empirical tests in 20 countries. *Advances in Experimental Social Psychology, 25*, 1–65.

Singh, L. (2012). Asbestos killed this man. Are you safe? https://www.mamamia.com.au/asbestos-warning-for-homerenovators-as-the-block-is-back-on-tv/

Tariq, S., & Woodman, J. (2013). Using mixed methods in health research. *JRSM Short Reports, 4*(6), 2042533313479197. https://doi.org/10.1177/2042533313479197.PMID:23885291;PMCID:PMC3697857

CHAPTER 6

Results and Discussion

Abstract Divided into two parts, this chapter presents the results of the observational study. The data are presented in figures to complement the Code Sheet relied on in the observational study (presented in table form). Three key themes emerged as a result of critically assessing the show. First, there was a perception that administrative and lower-wrung interventions were inconsistently applied and monitored during the season. Secondly, a culture of alcohol at work was normalised. Thirdly, psychosocial hazard awareness was either inadequate or undervalued. The findings support a cultural bias argument that perceived low-risk workplace activities and unacceptable psychosocial behaviours were tolerated. This data gave the viewer the impression The Block projected a form of dissonance which trivialised the importance of certain HSW cognitions. If this has occurred, then any conflict or inconsistency between workers' beliefs, attitudes, or behaviours regarding health, safety, and wellbeing and what is reasonably expected of workers, at the workplace, should be addressed.

Keywords Alcohol · Stereotypes · Culture · Tangible risks · Intangible risks · Psychosocial hazards

INTRODUCTION

The results of content analysis for the 48 episodes are presented below. Figure 6.1 presents the first set of observations recorded. These are typically described as tangible in that they relate to visual matters capable of being physically described (e.g. not wearing PPE while undertaking work). The term tangible is not used to determine that unequivocally an incident or event has occurred. Rather it is used to describe the physical characteristic of the possibility of occurrence. Figure 6.2 provides an average for those types of events. Table 6.1 at the end of the proceeding section provides context to these events by briefly describing in chronological order, the time-stamped event/occurrence (the coding data).

Similarly, the same processes are applied for Figs. 6.3 and 6.4 and Table 6.1 respectively for intangible issues identified. The term intangible is used to describe the more social and psychosocial characteristics of the workplace matters identified (e.g. attitudes towards alcohol, aggressive behaviour or talking about personal attributes or characteristics).

Each episode contained trivialisation of incidents of actual or apparent workplace acts, omissions, conduct and behaviours capable of being classified as questionable workplace behaviour. Tables 6.1 and 6.2 contain lists of identifiable matters captured in the observations. As stipulated,

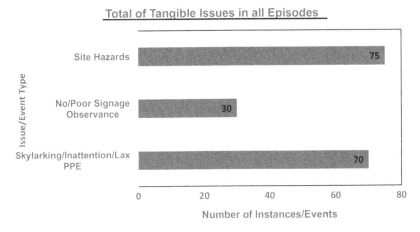

Fig. 6.1 Tangible issues—48 episodes where work was conducted

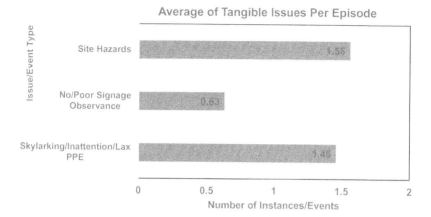

Fig. 6.2 Tangible issues—averaged per episode (48 episodes where work was conducted)

the coded data, especially concerning tangible observations may readily be explained (e.g. the item of plant caught on camera was temporarily placed or the site was about to be tidied up). The point of the observational study was to capture what was televised to the audience; or what was perceived to be something that might be reasonably queried by a viewer.

PART A: TYPOLOGIES 1,2 AND 3

First Typology: Skylarking/Inattention/Lax PPE

Figure 6.1 depicts the regularity of purported events. In every episode, there was evidence of visual display of what appeared to be intentional or inadvertent inappropriate onsite behaviour. It could be construed as silly or unprofessional behaviour. For example, George (H2) karate kicking old, fibrous wall sheeting without PPE[1] was a questionable act akin to skylarking. Skylarking (or horseplay) at the workplace was identified by the Court in *Newman v Andgra Pty Ltd* (2002) as a failure when an employer accepts the burden of permitting systems of work that allow for risk out of bravado; and in pursuit of "childish pleasure", such employees

---

[1] E2: 16:34.

engage in conduct which more mature staff would not. Recently it was observed employers were courting risk through horseplay and generally immature behaviour at a construction site by permitting such dangerous activity at a workplace (*Ajia v TJ & RF Fordham Pty Ltd [2020]*). It was obvious the light-hearted moments created useful footage for television, however George's method of work for demolishing sheeting was pointless and potentially risky for two reasons. The first is the likelihood of foreign bodies such as specks or fragments of building dust or fibre chips to the eye were reasonably high. The second is any loss of balance or footing could have resulted in George, who is of solid build, toppling onto the ground or the electrical hand tool to his left.

In another scene involving a nail gun, Daniel remarked, "Nails were flying everywhere. Old lad put them in upside down" and the admission that these tools were "kind of foreign", "funny" to George suggested not only playfulness, but lack of induction or training.[2] No one in that scene was wearing eye protection. This is concerning because the workers appeared to be using a Paslode 16 gauge angled nailer.

The instruction manual for this item of plant on p. 5 expressly provides (emphasis **not** added):

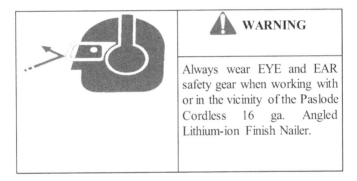

1. NEVER ASSUME THE TOOL IS EMPTY.
2. Never point the tool at yourself or anyone else.

---

[2] E1: 33:15–45.

NEVER ENGAGE IN "HORSEPLAY" WITH THE TOOL. The Cordless Finish Nailer is not a toy—it is a tool. Careless and improper use may result in a serious accident.

The above vignettes were confusing because the viewer was subjected to a form of risk trivialisation dissonance. On the one hand, these power tools on any assessment would be viewed as industrial items of plant; yet on the other hand, the viewer was subject to a level of playfulness concerning the use of these tools. This point is worth stressing because the media have made the connection between TV renovation shows and DIY injuries. Hamilton-Smith reported on a study in which "Dr Eley said DIY disasters from power tools have grown dramatically since the advent of home handyman TV shows. Injuries can be anything from a trivial laceration to a life-threatening event" (2016).

The risk of injury from skylarking has been discussed in case law and consumers are explicitly warned about horseplay in instructions manuals, but this behaviour has not received significant scholarly attention. Taking steps to educate any worker involved in skylarking and to train workers as to the need to eliminate or minimise the risk created by such behaviour was not depicted in the program. Supervisors did not appear to exercise control over the workers engaged in skylarking thereby displaying a permissive attitude towards it. Consider the scene in E26 where George (H2) entered a "wheelbarrow challenge" by racing up a plank (aluminium painter's style) with a wheelbarrow deliberately filled to the top with wet cement to make it difficult for him to push it up an incline (at 5:20):

Worker: *Right, there's one rule. You drop a wheelbarrow, you buy a slab [term used in Australia for a carton of beer]...that's for everyone*

George: *Yep...that's fair...I can live with that...everyone thinks I couldn't do it...not as easy as it looks. I had to run a full wheelbarrow up a three metre ramp [indicating with his hands the narrow width]...so they put that pressure on me again but they stitched me up as all Ollie's boys were getting half-filled barrows and mine was filled to the brim. The first two goes were perfect. And then one everyone started watching with the cameras I almost lost it. Got a neck injury...but I didn't drop any.*

Sarah: He would rather ruin his neck than pay for a slab of beer.

Playful antics aside, it should be stressed that the environmental conditions were wet potentially attracting slips, trips and falls hazards. Indeed, at one stage George did slip and drop down but to his delight, he exclaimed, "I didn't drop any" prompting his partner to make the neck remark above.

It is obvious the scene was designed for entertainment value, but from a safety perspective the above vignette can be broken down by way of the following syllogistic premise:

- <u>Work with a wheelbarrow is a work activity</u>

Major Premise: *Pushing a heavy object requires reasonable care and attention because the required physical exertion increases the risk of strain to the body, particularly the neck, back and arms.*
Minor Premise: *A wheelbarrow, when fully loaded, is a heavy object.*
Conclusion: *Therefore, pushing a fully loaded wheelbarrow in the absence of reasonable care and attention increases the likelihood of injury including strain to the body, particularly the neck back and arms.*

In Australia, the AIHS Body of Knowledge[3] specifically addresses issues concerning gravitational hazards and elements of hurrying, wet conditions, and slip, trips and falls; including wheelbarrow loads (Chapter 27, 2019). Whilst it is understood these vignettes were aired to captivate audiences with doses of humour and shenanigans for entertainment, the undertaking that was being promoted was work and that work forms an integral part of the construction process. The risk of serious neck injury from a resultant fall from the plank was actually identified by George's full and frank admission about the risk of injury. Yet it appears to have been trivialised in this scene as the central concern was not to lose the bet over a slab of beer.

---

[3] Australian Institute of Health and Safety publishes the Body of Knowledge as part of accreditation process.

In Chapter 27 of the BoK the authors observe:

> Despite this 'whole of life' exposure to fall hazards, there appears to be widespread complacency concerning the magnitude of the hazard, as reflected in the disproportionately low levels of coordinated governmental, community, and organisational preventative action directed at falls when compared to preventative measures relating to other hazards with higher profiles. (Adams, 2019: 2)

Following this line of reasoning, what if the subject matter related to work from height? Consider the following syllogistic premise:

- Work from height is a high-risk work activity

Major Premise: *Working at height requires tangible fall arrest protection because it poses a significant risk of falls from height*

Minor Premise: *Falls from height are a leading cause of serious injuries and fatalities at the workplace.*

Conclusion: *Therefore, working at height is a high-risk work activity and likelihood of serious injury* or death is high in the absence of fall from height protection.

The latter is immediately elevated to high-risk work activity as high-risk construction work generally includes involves a risk of a person falling more than 2 metres (e.g. see *OHS Regulations Victoria 2017* and all other WHS laws throughout Australia for that matter). It would be unimaginable how anyone could trivialise work at height given the high rate of fatalities. According to SWA, falls from heights are the leading cause of death at work (SWA, 2020).[4] Yet racing up a plank with a wheelbarrow laden with wet concrete was tolerated and seen as a worksite game for a bet on cartons of beer. Notwithstanding George was at an incline when he slipped with the wheelbarrow, he did leave the ground

---

[4] Working from heights is the leading cause of death and serious injury in Australia (Safe Work Australia, 2021), and from 2015–19, 122 fatalities from falls from heights (13 per cent of all fatalities) were recorded. Workers most at risk were those in the construction industry (WorkSafe, Queensland, 2021).

when he slipped, and technically he was not at ground level. Regulators throughout Australia have emphasised that *Slipping, tripping and ultimately falling from any height, can result in short to long-term injuries, even death* (SafeWork NSW, 2023). The point made here is not that George was in catastrophic danger, but rather, there would be zero tolerance for skylarking at significant height for obvious reasons. But if George did injure his neck, then the possibility of workers' compensation could not be excluded from such an eventuality.

Electrical Fires Are Not Entertainment: What's So Funny About Episode 23 (2:50–5:30)?

Collins (2024) has reported on a personal injuries matter currently before the County Court in Melbourne in which a tradesperson (Leigh Roberts) was employed to perform electrical work on House 3 of Season 17 of The Block. The claim concerns an allegation of sustaining electrical shock from conducting work on the show. Inter alia, injuries particularised include "stress, anxiety and depression" (Collins, 2024). The particulars according to this report revolve around working in or around electrical leads (Collins, 2024). As this matter is before the court, it is not the appropriate forum here to discuss whether or not a duty of care has been breached. But Mr Robert's injury is made in the context of the bizarre trivialisation of an electrical incident that resulted in a fire in Season 16. Extraordinarily this scene was exploited for entertainment, notwithstanding the potential seriousness of the incident:

Cam Scott: And Harry burns down his house!
H: I saw a flash; what's going on, and then lights went out. I could smell something in the air, something not quite right. We've lost power. I turned the corner. Flame! And it was getting bigger. An electrical flame. Jesus. I turn the corner, there's fire fire! Get the security to call the fire brigade. And I ran to where the fire was. Next thing I know George.
George: I heard everyone screaming fire. So we ran over. Are you right Harry?
Harry: I blew it (making a blowing sound).

> *The entire vignette was completely trivialised, replete with War of the Worlds soundtrack as Harry is portrayed a superhero. Yet the footage depicted extensively damaged socket outlet with clearly visible fire damage.*

Harry's daughter found the entire incident hysterical as contestants continued to laugh about "power box" fire.

Extraordinarily, Sarah's wife explained:

S:	Well what happened was Harry was about to touch the electrical that had just been on fire.
H:	George kicked me, if get electrocuted may get a glove
G:	Don't do it Harry, Don't do it
Natasha:	Dad maybe don't touch it.

George who is a qualified electrician then proceeded to take action. He advised the fault had tripped all the way back to the main switchboard near the street.

> *George*: So we had to go and find the key, open the doors switch everything back on and make it safe.

It is difficult to construe what unfolded in this episode as anything other than an electrical incident capable of causing serious and significant personal or property damage. Yet the incident was reduced to a silly sketch intertwined with serious factual ingredients. The facts are irrefutable. The footage depicted a fire-damaged temporary electrical distribution board. If it is accepted there was fire (which appears evident) then the following questions by the audience can objectively be asked:

- Was George qualified to take the relevant remedial action to make safe?
- What if George was not there and Harry touched the wiring?
- What if nobody was there and the fire grew?
- What if a Jetfire and LPG cylinder were nearby?

None of the above questions are misguided given the serious nature of electrical safety concerns generally. Yet the incident was overtly trivialised providing the audience with a downplayed sense of seriousness of the matter. Several observations were identified about Jetfire gas-fired electrical heaters being positioned in certain places in the context of a systems thinking approach (see Table 6.1). Taking a whole design approach and learning from the electrical fire described above, systems thinking addresses reductionist thinking and minimises risk trivialisation (see Flood & Jackson, 1991). For example, the consequential flow of an explosion would clearly be described as a critical incident had a Jetfire gas heater been in close proximity that night. By way of illustration, this vignette could have been an opportunity to reconfigure attitudes a whole of systems thinking approach, and prompt a consideration of organisational response to a consistent policy on say, Jetfire heater storage, or other items of plant for that matter. Such an observation is obviously speculative, but the seriousness of an electrical fire event should have been clarified to the viewer.

Lax PPE: Harden up Mate and Man It out George!

As this research focuses on perceptions of risk and how some things are trivialised, take the approach to George's splinter injury during E7. The incident required medical intervention; yet curiously it was seen as a light-hearted matter by all parties; not least of all, by the injured person, narrator Scott Cam and Dan the supervisor:

Scott Cam (SC):	*But the big build has produced a casualty*
Sarah (S):	*This morning there was a very big scenario*
George (G):	*I think my finger's infected…I was demoing the other day and I got a splinter. I tried to man it out and I woke up this morning and I couldn't close my finger. I've got a splinter and it's getting infected*
Natasha:	*Do you know what you need to put on it.*
G:	*Windex…got any*
SC:	*Not the best medical advice (a meme 'As sanctioned by Donald Trump Don't use Windex as a healing agent. That's insane, complements this narration). Best to take yourself to the medical centre George conveniently located across the road.*

G: *That was terrible.. was very painful was infected…bit sore but I am alive. That's the main thing.*

George then proceeded to joke about the size of the splinter and banter ensued with others about pus and nearly losing his arm and getting a tetanus shot.

G: *So I was I also showing Scotty my battle scar.*
SC: *Where's the scar…you've got a bandage on it (Scotty is laughing). Scott Cam then proceeds to compare his stitches from all the injuries he received and when his finger came off and so on.*
G: *I tried to toughen it out but I thought my finger had to be amputated (see generally E7: 21:54–24:30).*

However, the vignette did garner media attention. It was reported that George explained:

I honestly didn't want the crew to come with me. I told them, 'I know this is great TV but my finger is actually infected,' and I remember they were pretty good — they could see it was serious so they just let me go and. (Lyall, 2020)

The incident was trivialised for over 2 minutes and 30 seconds in E7 and the entire context was premised on the following:

a. The injury was minor;
b. The injured worker was prepared to "man it out"; and
c. The entire worksite dismissed the injury as trivial and jokes about the perceived silliness of the injury were exchanged;

Yet the reality was that 32-year-old George did receive medical attention because he was in pain and could not close his finger. The medical attention was at a medical centre where surgical intervention included cleaning the wound, dressing it for sterilisation and receiving a tetanus shot. According to Gullamhussein et al. (2016), tetanus infection can be severe and potentially fatal because it contains the bacterium *Clostridium tetani*. The authors present a case study of a 35-year-old sheet metal worker who presented with a swollen right thumb. He was eventually diagnosed with localised tetanus due to working on the factory floor.

Relevantly, for this scenario in E7, it is worth citing the case note in that study:

> *He recalled that 2 weeks ago, he had been injured with a metal splinter that he was able to extract it using a needle; however, the wound became infected. It discharged pus for a few days, and then seemingly resolved of its own accord, so he did not seek help.* (2016: 101)

The issue is not the injury per se, and whether it was a superficial and therefore a minor injury. Rather it is about whether or not George was wearing adequate PPE in the first instance or any relevant PPE for that matter. Could the infection have been prevented? As the first episode revealed the site was dirty (obviously), and airborne contaminants and contagious nanoparticles would be present. But equally relevant was the attitude displayed by all parties about the nature of injury. The level of risk trivialisation dissonance was clearly high. Yes, George was not diagnosed with having contracted tetanus, but his finger was sore, and he was going to continue to ignore it. Fortunately, he did not, and but for what appears to have been comprehensive medical attention, the scenario may not have been as trivial as played out in this vignette. It is fair to speculate given that his finger was infected and that the situation could have been more serious. In other words, this was not a case of a simple first-aid response. This injury required surgical intervention and according to the show, George was at the surgery for one hour.

Alternatively, it may be the case that George's infected finger was dramatised for television and it was not injured. This is highly unlikely given that the medical centre was depicted in the scene above and the show spent a significant amount of screen time portraying the injury. The likely conclusion is that this type of injury was dismissed as trivial despite it posing a potentially serious hygiene issue.

Considering George had thought to "man it out", the scene is indicative of stereotypical workplace culture. Coupled with banter and teasing around George's injury, "man it out" is an antiquated or archaic term to mean "brave it out" by playing a "manly part" and "bear one's self stoutly and boldly" (Century Dictionary, 1890). The observation is made in the setting of a construction site and to be man about it is a stereotype about the type of worker employed in construction. As the building industry is overwhelmingly male-dominated, for example of the 15% of women in construction less than 5% are blue collar, that is "on the tools"

(CSQ: 2021), such antiquated and trivial attitudes do little to positively promote an industry and where to "man it out" is a pointless attitude. This scene supports the literature that in construction workers take risks and "endure pain without complaint" and "often trivialise poor health and avoid help-seeking" (Galea et al., 2022).

THIS IS REALITY TV SO HARDEN UP MATE!

The reader may perhaps be wondering why is it important to only focus on matters deemed to be at the lower end of the harm scale. Issues identified or concerned with lower order controls such as adequate PPE adherence are hardly *prima facie*, life-threatening. Pushing wheelbarrows immaturely or receiving splinters are hardly life-threatening exposures. After all, signage languishing on the floor, banter at the worksite about male leg waxing and male modelling, or desperately expressing the need for wine are hardly comparable to serious injury or death. Indeed, the reader might be wondering whether the author should "harden up mate" or "toughen up" (as the phrases are used on Australian worksites).[5] To "harden up" on a building site is suggestive of a work culture where workers are expected to "man up", be tough and just get on with the job. The expression is analogous to a type of male-dominant construction culture presumably because the nature of the work is "hands-on" in a blue-collar environment where workers are expected to be brave. The incident described on The Block with George (H2) "manning it out" is an example of this attitude. Indeed, one wonders what may have happened if George did man it out and did not seek medical attention. O'Brien et al. (2005) make the link in their research that masculinity and not seeking assistance at work are causally connected. This reluctance to deviate from communicating issues is a universal theme in construction (Rochelle, 2019). Fortunately, George did go to a doctor and was not sent back to work until the required surgical intervention including vaccination for tetanus was administered.

This scenario is restated in this section because it is important to recognise that modern WHS legislation is not necessarily concerned with

---

[5] Brianna Fields in her article "Toughen Up Mate: The harmful effects of toxic masculinity on Australian men" (2024) provides an informative account of toxic masculinity on construction sites and mental health risks associated with men perpetuating toxic gender norms

whether actual harm has eventuated. Rather, the law is designed to protect against exposure to likelihood of death, serious injury or illness (see s. 32 of the *Model WHS Act 2011*). Exposure to risk is legally just as relevant as harm caused at work. In other words, the correct course of action was for George to query the injury itself and not "harden up mate". After all, it was just a splinter, a simple wound. Perhaps nothing would have flowed from the infection, or perhaps if not treated properly, the tiny wound could have become a serious health risk because germs entering the blood stream could cause infection which might lead to sepsis. The audience (thankfully) does not need to wonder because George sought medical assistance. He communicated the problem and consulted with staff. But he did think about "manning it out".

Australasian popular culture imbues itself on notions of mateship and loyalty, and this socio-political idea of mateship is extended to construction sites where workers are seen as knockabout, at times gruff, laid-back "Aussies" who say "G'day" to one another as they get on with physical work (Duarte et al., 2008). Indeed, Jasmin (H5) corroborated this iconic imagery of the working-class man (as immortalised in popular culture by the likes of former tradesman turned actor Paul Hogan and rock bands such as Cold Chisel) in one scene when she counselled the distraught Sarah (H3) that this is what tradies are like on worksites (see scenario below where Sarah confronted a male plasterer). The scene in which Sarah was allegedly sworn at was simply toxic, and could potentially be construed as aggression at work and subject to formal investigation. Yet there was no indication to the viewer whether the matter was dealt with adequately or not.

It seems this idea to harden up mate is akin to being physically (and probably mentally) strong. One should put up with it, and stay quiet so as to avoid being ridiculed at the worksite. This observation is made in the context of an advertisement in New Zealand narrated by The Block Host Scott Cam on behalf of Bisley Workwear (which is a significant sponsor of The Block). The Advertising Standards Authority (ASA) upheld a complaint made by a viewer complainant about the inappropriate portrayal of a workplace activity and subsequent incident at a construction site (ASA, 2017). The summary of the facts is as follows:

Description of Advertisement
The television advertisement for Bisley Workwear shows a series of mishaps on a building site. A bag of concrete mix breaks open over a worker's face,

a colleague cleans him off with water while saying "Harden up mate". The worker has dust blown into his face, with his colleague commenting "Bit dusty there buddy?" A pipe slips and pours water over the worker eating lunch. The co-worker say "Pipe down pal." Finally, the same worker has a bird poop" on his head, with the last comment being, "Looks like it's your lucky day." The advertisement ends with the tag-line, Bisley Workwear, we've got you covered.

The Complaint from J Lett

I'm concerned that this ad shows a tradie (not wearing safety glasses) getting a face full of what appears to be dry concrete or cement powder, being hosed in the face by another man and being told to "harden up. These building materials are extremely caustic and can cause serious eye damage. Although the appropriate initial treatment IS to wash out with copious water, any tradie should know this is potentially an emergency and they should seek urgent medical assessment, not "harden up".

The Complainant was concerned about the health and safety aspect of showing a worker having dry cement powder thrown in his face. As this substance can be caustic, they did not believe that it should be part of an attempt at a humorous scenario, centred around the pun "harden up".

The Advertiser's Response

The Advertiser confirmed that the advertisement was a light-hearted commercial showing over exaggerated building site incidents. They explained that the advertisement was filmed in a controlled environment using cosmetic powder. The substance was immediately washed off. The Advertiser did not consider it realistic that the worker unloading the cement bags would have been wearing protective goggles. The company stressed that they take health and safety seriously.

Bizarrely the scenes were reminiscent of absurd vignettes depicted in Abbott and Costello or Three Stooges style slapstick humour, and the defence justifications were intriguing. The company justified its actions by submitting the filming conditions were controlled and therefore safe. This misses the point of the complaint entirely in that the complaint was concerned with audience perception of what was being depicted. That is, the "properties of concrete contain Calcium Oxide which becomes Calcium Hydroxide when wet, making it an alkaline substance which can burn eyes and skin" (ASA, 2017).

The ASA was satisfied that any light-hearted depiction concerning inadvertence around handling substance caustic in nature elevated "safety mishaps" into a more "serious health and safety concern" (2017). Significantly, the ASA agreed that the play on the words "Harden up" was problematic "as it could be seen to **trivialise** the serious health risk concrete exposure to the skin and eyes could cause and imply the worker should simply ignore the incident and 'get over it'" (ASA, 2017). Findings by this authority are consistent with research into misguided male masculinity at building and construction sites (Rochelle, 2019) about the need to simply harden up and get on with the job, and thereby demonstrate physical or manly strength by not complaining about matters at work (Galea et al., 2022).

The defendant advertiser persisted with some force and attempted to unsuccessfully defend the allegation by submitting the incident exaggerated, that "harmless cosmetic powder" was used in a "controlled environment" and curiously in "real life" this would "most probably be a small amount of dirt". Bisley then explained that they "do like to take a humorous approach to promoting ourselves". But perhaps the most confusing submission was that Bisley felt J. Lett's suggestion of wearing goggles whilst unloading a vehicle would occur in a practical environment, was in the premises, unrealistic. This justification is both questionable and contradictory because images clearly depicted a bag of fine dry powder torn and its contents airborne so as to come in contact with the manual handler's face and eyes. Yet in a subsequent image, the worker was then wearing goggles. In any event any assessment as to whether or not the activity was unrealistic with goggles on or not is a regulatory matter subject to New Zealand's *Health and Safety at Work (Hazardous Substances) Regulations 2017*. But one would reasonably suspect that toxic materials, containing crystalline silica for example, capable of escaping its packaging should be handled with appropriate PPE. Furthermore, Bisley provides workwear and is not involved in cement handling activities. No expert evidence was adduced about the safe handling of cement. In the premises, the complainant was entitled to call out such trivialisation of a potentially serious matter.

INADVERTENCE AND INCONSISTENT SIGNAGE OBSERVANCE

King describes acts of inattentiveness as unreasonably risky, or careless, thoughtless conduct capable of causing negligent acts or omissions and is essentially a conscious or unconscious failure to consider the risk (2009: 578). Inattention, inadvertence or negligence on the part of the employee presents a cluster of risks an employer is required to guard against (*Mantica v Coalroc [2022]*). Yet in the very first episode contestants were provided with various items of plant including angle nail guns, electric saws, hammers and chisels as work was being performed in the absence of particular PPE in circumstances where PPE must be worn. The subject of discussion below, is an individual (Daniel, H3) who was filmed standing behind signage but was not wearing relevant PPE as depicted in the sign.[6] Similarly, when Mitre Rob delivered a white board to Daniel in E18[7] both were standing next to or around what appears to be a *Head Protection Must Be Worn In This Area* sign.

These observations are not made to suggest signs are capable of physically minimising the risk. They are ranked at the lower end of control procedures. However, signs, inter alia, are capable of educating workers, for example, that head protection is designed to protect workers if there is a risk that they could be struck on the head by falling objects. The viewer knows this risk was likely because construction work was being undertaken from all directions as was evident by the sound of hammering, drilling and associated noise. In one episode workers were directed by Foreperson Keith (K) to put on a hard hat. In that incident K explained a "piece of timber just missed the plumber's head...when V Lux are working, we've gotta have helmets on...on the Block the most important thing is safety, it didn't happen, it was stupid...and it's not going to happen again". As a consequence, the incident was reported by K to James the OH&S Enforcer who re-inducted workers for House 3 as it was "shutdown pending an investigation".[8] But in the same episode, at Jimmy's house (No. 5),[9] K performed a site visit in which workers were undertaking similar tasks as above. What was curious was that no direction was given to Jimmy and his workers to wear a hard hat. A reasonable

[6] E1: 33:19.
[7] At 8:58.
[8] E5: 30:35–32:10.
[9] At 36:38.

inference drawn here is that unless there was an actual event, there was no HSW issue. This approach is inconsistent with the regulatory position as the purpose of HSW is to minimise *exposure* to harm or the *likelihood* of harm (see s. 5 and 32 of *Work Health and Safety Act 2011*). A potential risk is just as significant as an actual event where an incident has materialised.

The fact that Foreperson K was silent on the issue of Jimmy's workers not wearing a hard hat was confusing. Such silence can be construed as perceived cultural bias because it was immaterial that there was no incident. Cognitively, it was of less importance, and subsequently trivial.[10] The hard hat rule should have been enforced in both circumstances; irrespective of an actual, near or theoretical incident. The law is unequivocal about the fact a consequence leading to a circumstance of aggravation (that is an actual injury) is not the point of WHSW. Rather the purpose of WHSW is to minimise exposure through an integrated and holistic approach for reduced harm (Karanikas et al., 2022). Signage observance and PPE play a part in this goal and accordingly, the perceived level of inconsistency suggests bias about the effectiveness of interacting low order controls on the show by virtue of cognitive dissonance.

The inconsistent use and enforcement of PPE as depicted in the signs on The Block supports the commonly held view in various industries including construction that individual and organisational factors determine use of PPE (James et al., 2023). It is not known whether use of PPE may not have been comprehensively monitored due to discomfort or lack of training or awareness, or production pressures discouraged its use due to PPE slowing workers (Sasangohar et al., 2018). It was obvious PPE was worn during the season. However, data presented in the tables below support the observation workers faced sustained increased workload pressures to meet room reveal deadlines. It is open to speculation whether a *consistent* approach to PPE enforcement was presented on the show. The purpose of these observations is not to be antagonistic or alarmist about non-conformism in relation to low order controls such as signage and PPE. It is presented to posit that it is arguable these considerations were deemed likely to be trivialised in the circumstances presented in the footage.

---

[10] E5: 36:55.

In a concerning scene, Jasmin (H4) inadequately secured a coffee table and chair; and this unsecured load fell from the back of her moving vehicle onto the middle of a designated road.[11] This scene clearly provided rich content for producers to highlight the naivety or perhaps inexperience of the featured contestant workers (e.g. not knowing how to use a nail gun or joking and creating a funny sketch about an actual electrical fire).[12] The reality is these events are inherently dangerous. Unsecured loads have been the subject of parliamentary inquiries. Consider the following observations by the Queensland Parliament:

> Unsecured and improperly secured loads on vehicles are a serious road safety hazard for all road users. Over the years, many people have been killed and injured as a result of load related accidents (1997, Preface); and

> Unsecured load materials hauled by private and commercial vehicles can expose road users to significant hazards...A shifting load may cause the driver to lose control of the vehicle resulting in a crash. Loads that are not properly secured or covered and fall from vehicles onto roads pose a further hazard to other road users that is exacerbated by high travelling speeds and traffic volumes. (1997, 26)

The point made here about this overtly inattentive scene is that Jasmin whilst not onsite, was conducting work, and the workplace was a moving vehicle in addition to the system of work surrounding collecting and loading material onto the back of the vehicle. This incident occurred on a designated road thereby aggravating the potential for harm due to a potentially serious roadway safety risk. Yet the seriousness of this work-related incident matter was subsumed by the actions of a stranger who purportedly attempted to keep this fallen bounty of goods belonging to Jasmin. The overshadowing of a safety concern caused, presumably by undue care, inattention or inadvertence is a good example of risk trivialisation as the incident was downplayed.

In the scene above it is not so much that something fell from the back of a car. Things do fall, and YouTube is replete with programmes devoted

---

[11] E48: 11:20.
[12] Refer to Table 6.1 and E1 and E23 respectively.

to these mishaps.[13] Similarly, when landscaper Dave Franklin was eating McDonalds fries whilst barely connecting to the steering wheel in Episode 46, the observation was noted not because there is a Victorian road rule that stipulates eating and driving is illegal. The author is not being angelic about this motoring behaviour. But quite frankly, Franklin was working, and his workplace was a motor vehicle; and it is reasonable to infer talking to George whilst eating and driving would be deemed as common in-vehicle distractions. The worker must ensure proper control of the vehicle so as to avoid an allegation of exposure to dangerous or careless driving. In other words, pursuant to Victoria's' *Occupational Health and Safety Act 2004* driving is a work-related duty, and that law reminds PCBUs (employers) that work-related driving is considered work and that obligations arise from such work. The Regulator explains "A culture of safety recognises that the driving task is often a much higher risk that needs to be managed closely". Yet Jasmin and Dave and Franklin's vignettes are trivial in depiction.

Inconsistent use of PPE, inattention or skylarking around items of plant and equipment are matters pertaining to supervision at the workplace which are generally administrative in nature. Re-enforcement of worksite administration appeared to be a low order priority at this site.[14] It is perhaps likely workers' behaviours in terms of PPE compliance, inadvertence and skylarking were related to the workplace atmosphere on the show's construction site. In line with CRT, the rate of frequency of not adhering to low order controls suggested these practices were not perceived as dangerous. Furthermore, the footage depicting lax PPE practice suggested underestimation of work hazards, or bravado or over-confidence when performing repetitive tasks at the workplace. As mentioned above, the ASA (NZ) upheld a complaint about an advertisement starring host Cam Scott in which skylarking and lax PPE were depicted. The ASA affirmed the depictions as dangerous practices which encouraged a disregard for safety. A light-hearted approach to an image of cement dusted being blown in the face of a worker or a focus on Jasmin retrieving her goods from a person are examples of dissonance through

---

[13] See Dash Cam Owners Australia https://www.youtube.com/c/dashcamownersaustralia.

[14] Another example in E46 at 9:09 where MANDATORY PPE sign is being ignored by some not wearing Hi-Viz.

the process of trivialisation. These narratives mask the serious underlying WHSW themes by entertaining viewers with shenanigans or mishaps.

Construction site safety rules displayed on approved signage, designed to depict best practices, are commonly placed on construction sites.[15] Safety Signs (like PPE) are classed as low order/wrung administrative control measures and universally accepted as obvious low-cost ways to warn anyone who may come into contact with a hazard (Code of Practice, 2021: 20). It is trite to emphasise the importance of safety signs in safety management systems as these displayed warnings provide signals and alert individuals to hazardous situations and provide visual information that helps to avoid harm (Ayres, 2013).

Thirty observations throughout the entire season concerned potential non-observance or lack of signage consideration. Ignoring signage or demonstrating ambiguous or arbitrary signage observance suggested this administrative process was inconsistently applied on The Block. It is likely the reason for non-observance was because there was no meaningful cognitive safety prioritisation placed on the importance of signage. Alternatively, the workers did not understand the significance of these messages and placed low value on signage. Despite the existence of clear signs, signage adherence appeared to be ambiguous or dissonant. It is likely the relevance of signage was perceived as a low order priority and beliefs and attitudes attached to signage support the argument that signs at workplaces are seen as trivial modes of information facilitation (Conzola & Wolgater, 2001). The data demonstrate despite the fact signs appeared to be placed throughout the entire site, it is difficult to determine whether safety behaviour was modified at the individual level. This was evidenced by the fact workers appeared non-compliant in front of visibly displayed signage. This was also apparent with purported non-observance of social distancing signage at the height of the pandemic on occasion. Viewers were advised of the COVID-19 protocols in place but it was unclear to what extent these signs were effective.

---

[15] See for example Australian Standard 1319–1994 (AS 1319). It outlines the need to devise and implement safety signs in a work environment to ensure safe workplace behaviour and practices and hazards prevention.

Site Hazards: Clutter, Mess and Poor Food Hygiene Examples

In the third tangible hazards category, messy sites featured prominently (75 events) or at the rate of 1.46 per episode and this included occasions of unhygienic food practices. Clutter, untidy or generally messy worksites have generally been viewed as inviting potential slip, trip and fall hazards. The Court has viewed a site in an unclean condition could constitute a tripping hazard and result in an injury to persons at the workplace (*The DoubleTree Hilton Case [2021]*). Liy et al. (2017) observe poor site housekeeping are common construction hazards. The Block on a number of occasions featured scenes of dangling cables on walls and floors and strewn materials, and plant and equipment in environments where several workers were crammed in one space.[16]

Rigorous scholarship on tidy sites is uncommon in the literature. Haslam et al., (2005: 410) revealed the proximate nexus between untidy sites and injury at construction sites in their research. They conclude, "Workplace factors, most notably poor housekeeping and problems with the site layout and space availability, were considered to have contributed in half (49%) of the accident studies. Aboagye-Mino and Emuze (2007: 2027) have expressly researched site hazards and the likelihood of harm caused by slips, trips and falls proximately associated with "uneven ground", untidy sites, mess, tools, materials and items of plant left on the ground and mussy conditions. Table 6.1 particularises environmental conditions that were consistent with the dangers identified by these authors. Harry's injury described below is not uncommon at workplaces generally. To that end, it is noted that in the 2023 season of The Block, a contestant worker stepped backwards and fell through penetration on the floor as it had not been secured. It was reported that "Bathroom week has begun and with it the dreaded 'waterproof Wednesday' is not far off, and the contestants are so stressed they're falling through holes in the floor and crashing cars" (Demarco, 2023). The couple explained that "people were using the manhole for running pipes beneath the floor but someone

---

[16] It must be emphasised a cable depicted dangling in an isolated image is not dangerous per se. However, dangling leads combined with leads on the floor and clutter on the ground could potentially attract a hazard. A system of work which is neat and tidy is indicative of housekeeping designed to avoid a slip, trip or fall.

had left it uncovered". The technical term for this is an unsecured penetration and codes of practice exist to ensure the likelihood of such falls are prevented e.g.:

> Protection around holes, penetrations and openings
> A fall prevention device (for example, cover) must be used to provide and maintain a safe system of work where persons are working near and around holes, penetrations and openings through which a person could fall, if it is reasonably practicable to do so. (Code of Practice, 2021: 22)

Extraordinarily, in 2022, contestant Jenny also explained how she fell through deck joints, and this was "horrific". She described falling straight down and was bleeding and swollen. She sustained injuries as a consequence of the joists (Lowther, 2022). In this research, the practice of straddling was observed throughout the show (see e.g. E6 and 33). Again the point of identifying the risk is not to point out injuries that were sustained (they clearly were). Rather it is to highlight the perception that harm or likelihood of harm might arise from potentially lower risk activities such as slips, trips and falls.

CLUTTER AND HOUSEKEEPING: IT'S ALL FUN AND GAMES UNTIL HARRY BREAKS A BONE ON UNEVEN GROUND

Popular media outlets reported an injury during the filming of Season 16. *New Idea* (2020) described the "perfect storm of fatigue combined with a hazardous environment" led a contestant to "suffer injury" in circumstances surrounding walking and wet surfaces. The injury related to Harry (H1) who was nicknamed "Dirty Harry" as a consequence of sneaking around the site during lockdown. Consider the news report about a slip, and Harry limping. Harry described the circumstances as follows[17]:

H: *In my haste and rush to get the room finished, I stood on a piece of uneven piece of ground and I rolled my ankle. Yeah I sprained it. I am immobile. I can't do anything which I feel really bad for Natasha and everyone else who now have to support me while I get this sorted...probably get*

---
[17] E13 (32:02).

	an X-ray to see if I haven't broken anything; see if it's just ligaments, I think it's ligaments.
Scott Cam (SC):	*Until Harry can get to the doctors for an X-ray he's gonna be flat out working from their bedroom.*
H:	*I am gonna sit down and just supervise the trades from the master because of my I can't put boots on so I need to be careful about what I do.*
Foreperson Dan (FD):	*Where is everyone? Do we know?*
SC:	*Harry's missing because he has been at the doctors getting an X-ray on his injured foot*
H:	*The doctor had me X-rayed to see exactly what was going on…I need to got emergency tonight…and um hopefully they can fit me in moon boot…I will be restricted. My foot is broken and I have to stay off it…crutches…-moon boot.*
FD:	*No different to the last three or four weeks let's be honest he didn't do too much he pretty just organised so instead being in the room he is just doing it in the bed…I am being honest it's no different from any other week.*

There are several concerns about the way this scene unfolded. First, by way of setting the scene, the conditions in which the incident occurred included a work site with power tools and various items of plant, debris and materials strewn on the so-called "uneven piece of ground". In other words, access in and around the workplace generally was very cluttered. For example, around what appears to be a walk path, there were uneven pieces of sheeting, bits of wood and objects on the ground. Working in and around this mess including loose cable and leads on the ground, ladders or trestles dropped in front of a fire extinguisher, ladders and unsecure items of scaffolding precariously leaning against the edge of a small tin roof, prima facie, did not appear safe in the premises. It is difficult to conceptualise how the state of the site could be deemed acceptable for construction workers in circumstances where there are several individuals onsite. Based on this scene with Harry, is it reasonable to raise questions about whether the system of work under which the contestants were working, was ideal? That is, should it not be obvious to the producers that deadlines and same-day delivery of materials would lead to cluttering and storage issues creating the risk of slips, trips and falls? Additionally, given the onsite mess, would a reasonable person accept the proposition an individual is likely to slip, trip or fall on uneven ground? The answers could be answered in the affirmative.

But the issue in the above vignette is not that a serious injury occurred per se. Injuries at the workplace occur, and this incident gained media attention because of that newsworthy event. Rather, an inference could be drawn about whether the duty holder had taken appropriate steps to assess and manage the risk of injury arising from work conditions having regard to the cluttered nature of the work spaces and sites. Another point that should be raised in this scene is the psychosocial nature of the injury. Harry, the injured worker felt "really bad" because he was letting his daughter and team down; despite the fact he had a sore foot; something significantly more serious than just a roll or sprain. There was a perception that this incident caused great inconvenience despite the fact Harry placed himself on light organisational duties. Light duties assignment would be unremarkable in any return-to-work setting. What was remarkable is that the Foreperson Dan belittled Harry's course of action given that in the previous Episode (11) he was berated for not adequately project managing.

Luke the Chippy or Luke the Chef?

As messy and cluttered sites also potentially attract hygiene issues, it was difficult to ascertain whether hand hygiene was consistently practised on the show. The show depicted workers practising poor food hygiene, for example, eating pizza on the floor near dirty work boots or supervisors eating cakes whilst handling materials.[18] In one scene Luke (H4) used a saw to cut bread and served an antipasto meal on off-cut building material resting on a tub.[19] Despite the fact food and beverage consumption played a prominent feature on the show, there were incidents of questionable food handling and consumption practices that were patently

---

[18] E23: 49:38 and E5: 39:42.
[19] E16: 20:30.

inconsistent with best practices for food hygiene (Buchtmann, 2021). The scene with Luke supports the concern raised in the codes around a "risk of substances or processes contaminating food" (Code of Practice, 2019: 23).

The rate of these events throughout the season supports the proposition that practice around site tidiness was perceived as low-risk matters by participants, and generally cognitively trivial. Perhaps the reason for this is that common sense dictates responsible adults would ensure proper site tidiness and food hygiene. The point here is not to infer serious illness or risk of spread of illness was observed. But this show was filmed at the height of the COVID-19 pandemic where several individuals frequented the site and matters of hygiene could be raised in the premises. There was no vaccine available and authorities had created guidance, namely; hygiene protocols including hand washing before eating and avoiding touching contaminated surfaces (SWA, 2020) (Table 6.1).

PART B: TYPOLOGIES 4,5 AND 6

Intangible Considerations: Social Environment, Culture and Psychosocial Concerns

In 2023, on the popular online news and opinion website, *MamaM!a* (Mamamia) the following headline appeared, "Why I will no longer watch this season of The Block". The writer Eva Farrell explained:

> *On Monday night we stopped watching renovation series, The Bullies…I mean…only six episodes into the latest season my daughter and I had seen more bullying than building, and we'd had enough.. So it's beyond me why The Block is promoting a toxic and disturbing bullying narrative…*

This opinion piece is not an isolated view and it echoes the sentiment of apparent "disgust" from popular Channel Nine media stars Hamish Blake and Andy Lee (Guertin, 2023). It is interesting that media personalities have reportedly seen fit to complain to senior executives of the Nine Network. The views of these charismatic personalities coincide with several media complaints to the commercial TV regulatory body (ACMA) with respect to complaints concerning the promotion of anti-social behaviour on The Block currently under review (Guertin, 2023). At the time of writing, a decision from the ACMA about the complaints has not been made; but the issue is not whether the complaints will be

Table 6.1 Season 16 (2020) The Block Observation: Code Book for Typologies 1, 2 & 3[20]

Episode	Skylarking, Lax PPE Usage/questionable methods/practices	Purported Lax/No PPE Signage/Instruction Observance	Site Appearance: Untidy, clutter, messy, pedestrian obstacles (slip/trip hazards), hygiene
1	"Nail gun—nails were flying everywhere... Old lad put them in upside down" (33:18–33:43) Power tool (nail gun) usage with no eye protection (31:42–33:53, 100:05–31)	Apparent lack of observance of "This protective equipment must be worn on this site" signage (e.g. 35:38 or 32:06)	All houses messy, dusty, cluttered and appear unhygienic (21:00) In this episode, participants walk through potentially hazardous worksite with no PPE (debris, unsecured door, unsecured ceiling fitting, rat skeleton (and Jimmy playfully touching it at 21:04) and pungent stench ("stinks like piss") (21:30–22). Impression: dirty, dusty, site potentially unhygienic practices and worksite. Query no PPE
2	H3: George karate kicks and pushes wall sheeting without eye protection (16:34)		

(continued)

---

[20] In the broader context of the system of work at the site.

Table 6.1 (continued)

Episode	Skylarking, Lax PPE Usage/questionable methods/practices	Purported Lax/No PPE Signage/Instruction Observance	Site Appearance: Untidy, clutter, messy, pedestrian obstacles (slip/trip hazards), hygiene
3	Query placement of LPG type cylinder indoors connected to 'Jetfire' type Kennards Hire gas electric heater around powered plant or equipment in 5 m room with unsecured electrical extension cord (15:45). Item is connected; cannot ascertain if on. Heater used typically for large industrial areas (and with use only in a well ventilated space warnings) (Note Energy Safe Victorian Regulator's advice about LPG appliances and "should never be used inside"). Jetfire manual does not specify indoor use; note manufacturer specifies *Their main applications include heating of warehouses, workshops, garages, factories, transport terminals, breeding sheds and greenhouses they can also be used for drying and curing materials in the building, agricultural and other industries, but not suitable for domestic use and when in use adequate fresh air ventilation must be provided (Industry Update, 2024)*. H1: Harry on phone having intense conversation and inattentively walking around fiddling with chisel whilst leaning on Bailey ladder with hammer precariously placed on top of ladder (40:38)	Appear to ignore hard hat area signage (safety helmets must be worn) (7:53 & 19:10)' i.e. This is a hard hat area, Safety helmets must be worn (George in front of signage 21:00)	H1 cluttered and messy worksite (45:53)

Episode	Skylarking, Lax PPE Usage/questionable methods/practices	Purported Lax/No PPE Signage/Instruction Observance	Site Appearance: Untidy, clutter, messy, pedestrian obstacles (slip/trip hazards), hygiene
4	Daniel (H3) and George(H2) not wearing gloves, long sleeves or eye protection during floor insulation (15:61 & 18:00)		
5	Worker demolishing floor with sledgehammer yet no eye protection, gloves or mask (6:28) H3: Squatting with back to a void at height whilst measuring with left hand and phone in other hand (8:48) Dramatisation of incident at Dan and Jade's house when a piece of timber fell from height and just missed the plumber's head without hard hat said Dan (30:40). Keith shuts site down for not wearing that PPE. All workers were re-inducted with respect to hard hat wearing (31:25) Query worker balanced with left foot on top cap of Bailey's ladder (42:36)	First time acknowledgement that hard hats must be worn at all times (32:08) [H3] What was not mentioned was Velux worker standing between two pieces of timber at height (30:00), worker hanging from frame at what appears to be at height (30:05) In same episode (H5) despite hard hat sign rule not being enforced hard hat is worn intermittently or on an ad hoc basis in H5 (36:47). Inconsistent rule enforcement presumably because scene was incident free	Supervisors Keith and Dan eating cakes whilst touching materials—query level of food safety and food habit (39:42)

(continued)

Table 6.1 (continued)

Episode	Skylarking, Lax PPE Usage/questionable methods/practices	Purported Lax/No PPE Signage/Instruction Observance	Site Appearance: Untidy, clutter, messy, pedestrian obstacles (slip/trip hazards), hygiene
6	Supervisor Keith straddling wooden frames when ply sheet on floor could be used (3:41) Two workers carrying a sheet whilst straddling wooden frames with exposed raised floor (20:00) Luke cutting cement fibre sheet with a grinder with no dust extraction (41:40)		H4: Untidy cluttered site (query potential for slip trip hazards) (7:24)
7	No visible use of eye protection by Luke with angle gun and other tools under house (3:55) and making light of George's splinter infection (H3 at 21:54–23:00)		Cable management query: Loose electrical cables dangling in walkway in H1 appear low—below Dan's head (12:14). Consider safety hooks to improve system for cabling Power pack with cables hanging—one cable stretched—no slack in H5 (32:47). Consider mounting bracket or hook for proper fit
8			

6 RESULTS AND DISCUSSION 89

Episode	Skylarking, Lax PPE Usage/questionable methods/practices	Purported Lax/No PPE Signage/Instruction Observance	Site Appearance: Untidy, clutter, messy, pedestrian obstacles (slip/trip hazards), hygiene
9	H4: Harry demolishing unsafely (nearly struck by ceiling and without eye protection, mask, gloves) (24:34 & 31:08); compare with H4 demolishing and appropriate PPE worn by Luke and Dan (29:01 or see 32:45) Five workers in and around industrial skip bin—some not wearing mask or eye protection—very dusty (35.08)—compare with H4, supervisor dramatically alerting workers to possible cement sheeting/asbestos and shutting work down—re-inducted. Identification of hazards inconsistent (37:10)		H4: Query angle of dangling power leads (entanglement) (31:41) H5: Appearance of untidy/cluttered site (46:30)
10	H4: Luke: emptying industrial vacuum cleaner without PPE (renovation dust, 14:59)—yet had been re-inducted about cement dust in E9 (15:03). Furthermore, the houses were in derelict state and by the foreperson's own observation throughout show, latent hazardous materials might reasonably be inferred as being in existence	H1: Ignoring hard hat sign/inconsistent hard hat usage (8:20, 9:12, 13:54, 15:32) H2: Ignoring hard hat sign/inconsistent hard hat usage (several workers for large ceiling rose removal but not re-installation) (26.05, 27.10)	

(continued)

Table 6.1 (continued)

Episode	Skylarking, Lax PPE Usage/questionable methods/practices	Purported Lax/No PPE Signage/Instruction Observance	Site Appearance: Untidy, clutter, messy, pedestrian obstacles (slip/trip hazards), hygiene
11	H2: Spray painting without mask (18:17)	Inconsistent use of Hi-Viz clothing by onsite visitors; walking around uncluttered site without PPE in contravention of signage (agents) (26:00–31:40, 35:13)	H2: George: query dangling, cable, untidy presentation (16:37) H3: Agent, Dan and jade using orange Bingo waste bin as desk; query cleanliness of bin (33:27)
12	H4 Luke: no PPE using bench saw (9:19)		H3, 1, 2: Query Dangling cables, (2:42, 7:12, 12:32) H1: Constant site clutter (13:04)

Episode	Skylarking, Lax PPE Usage/questionable methods/practices	Purported Lax/No PPE Signage/Instruction Observance	Site Appearance: Untidy, clutter, messy, pedestrian obstacles (slip/trip hazards), hygiene
13	H3: Query potential for hazard: Use of 'Jetfire' type heater blower appears to be in use in use positioned with LPG gas bottle indoors in corner (in ensuite) used with extension electrical cable on actual or near the heat source (4.22). Note: the heat sources are abutted in corner (1 m required) and surrounded by wood (combustible), the LPG gas cylinder is in front of the heat source, there is no front guard and a bottle of Dy Mark HIGHLY FLAMMABLE line marking paint is in apparent reasonable proximity to heat source. Note Jetfire instruction manual: *Keep combustible materials a safe distance from this unit (min 3 m and Use only in areas free from flammable materials (flammable vapours, high dust concentrations etc.) (p. 7)*		H1: cluttered and messy site, loose items scattered (9:42), Harry reveals in his haste he stood on uneven ground and injured himself—rolled it and thought he sprained it (10.00); foot is actually broken; has crutches, moon boot (32.02) H4: Dangling lead—use hooks, cable fasteners etc preferred. (47.12)
14	H1: Harry walking around cluttered site carrying sheeting board in moon boot (32.00)		H5: Clutter and H3: Query position of dangling lead (4.00–5.00)

(continued)

Table 6.1 (continued)

Episode	Skylarking, Lax PPE Usage/questionable methods/practices	Purported Lax/No PPE Signage/Instruction Observance	Site Appearance: Untidy, clutter, messy, pedestrian obstacles (slip/trip hazards), hygiene
15	Foreman/Supervisor Dan casually driving van with only one hand on the steering wheel whilst engaged in conversation (2:57) H3: using cordless drywall screwdriver contrary to operating instructions—no PPE and in haste to repair walls (8:58) H4: Luke cutting tiles using power tool but no mask (17:42)		
16	H4: query system of work for manual handling two people carrying 250 kg bath (18:02)		H4: Luke uses a saw to cut bread and serves antipasto meal on off cut material resting on wobbly board and tub. Tools strewn on floor (20:30) H5: Query dangling cable (10:17)
17	Rush to unpack deliveries yet hard hats rarely worn on construction site (26:17)	Non-observance of Covid distancing sign and generally difficult to ascertain social distancing (22:38, 38:14) H1: Harry repeatedly returned to site during lock down—against protocol—despite warning signage and now labelled "shifty/dirty Harry") (50:47)	Dangling cables/leads generally—hooks required (33:05)

Episode	Skylarking, Lax PPE Usage/questionable methods/practices	Purported Lax/No PPE Signage/Instruction Observance	Site Appearance: Untidy, clutter, messy, pedestrian obstacles (slip/trip hazards), hygiene
18	H5: inserting wall insulation without any PPE and H1: Lifting heavy plasterboard sheets upwards—no hard hat (31:50)	T1: Harry uses spray gun—no mask (PPE recommended see symbol on plant) (25:00)	Dangling cables query (7:59)—to be fastened? H4: Leads, tools lying on ground cluttered and obstacles (28:13)
19	H1: Query Harry spray painting without PPE (25:00, 27:00) H3: nail gun no eye protection (11:58)		Dangling cables: H4 (7:35, 7:53), H3 (29:12, 42:38), H5 (35:28), H2 (35:43, 44:37)
20	H4: bench saw no PPE (scene where everyone is rushing before tools down) (19:30)		H1: Clutter/messy site (38:33) H2: Stray power cord in doorway—potential trip; could be fastened H4: Query if low hanging power lead could be raised (6:56)
21	H3: Three workers on close proximity on ladders using nail guns to install ceiling sheeting—no eye protection H4: workers in close proximity using nail guns and other power tools—no eye protection (42:52)	H3: Ignoring/non-observant with regard to hard hat sign (32:51)	H5: Dangling lead—use hook (20:24) H3: Dangling lead (27:30, 28:30) H4: Dangling lead (42:44)

(continued)

Table 6.1 (continued)

Episode	Skylarking, Lax PPE Usage/questionable methods/practices	Purported Lax/No PPE Signage/Instruction Observance	Site Appearance: Untidy, clutter, messy, pedestrian obstacles (slip/trip hazards), hygiene
22	H4: Query social distancing/contact (2:42-53) compared to H3 (23:59). H2: Query indoor positioning and use of 'JetFire' LPG cylinder portable heater in rooms with electrical cord unsecured on floor (4:07), H3 (3:34 (in use) and positioned in messy area (23:53). H3: Screw gun use with no PPE (25:40)		H4: Low hanging/dangling lead (2:34) and H3: (7:11) and H3 and see 23:32 dangling lead is at neck and shoulder height to lift by hand to get through. H2: worksite clutter (37:56), H5 (42:21)
23	Trivialisation of electrical fire laughing and joking about the incident (2:50-5:50)		H4: Lead on floor should be secured (26:50). H3&1: Floor clutter (29:19). Luke: food hygiene—handling seafood with apparently bare hands appear to be dirty hands (48:15). Eating pizzas on floor, dirty work boots nearby (49:38)
24		Query COVID-19 Notice yet four in close proximity; handling raw food (possible cross-contamination) (13:48)	H3&4: Loose leads on ground as potential issue(5:49, 7:47 and carrying very heavy object; should secured. H4: clutter (12:16) and contrast food handler wearing gloves but workers eating around on worksite with hands (12:16)

Episode	Skylarking, Lax PPE Usage/questionable methods/practices	Purported Lax/No PPE Signage/Instruction Observance	Site Appearance: Untidy, clutter, messy, pedestrian obstacles (slip/trip hazards), hygiene
25	Lying down using pneumatic nail gun, no PPE (32:29)	H2 & H1: Despite signage at front of house, social distancing appears not to be observed (27:15, 28:22)	H2: Dangling lead query (22:23) H4: Leads on floor (32:29)
26	George running up with full barrows "got a neck injury" skylarking with concrete (5:20)	No social distancing query (11:08)	H4: Hanging lead in walkway (9:19)
27	Query whether hard hat should be worn—exposure to head injury from panel being lowered by crane on a roof (13:33)		
28	Worker drilling into ceiling—particles in air (no mask) (8:27)	No social distancing query (5:08); e.g. H3(16:51)—despite signage	H2: Clutter among hectic activity (5:04)
29	H2 George handling insulation with no gloves (but has mask) (45:28)		H2: Leads dangling—general cable management observation (9:53) H4: Leads dangling (29:17) H2: Leads dangling over latter (45:25) & see 46:04
30	Three workers all on ladders using powered nail/screw guns but no PPE (2:00) H4: no hard hats worn for work requiring PPE (19:15)		H5: Floor clutter and cables dangling (15:00)

(continued)

Table 6.1 (continued)

Episode	Skylarking, Lax PPE Usage/questionable methods/practices	Purported Lax/No PPE Signage/Instruction Observance	Site Appearance: Untidy, clutter, messy, pedestrian obstacles (slip/trip hazards), hygiene
31	H2: Query used of elevated wallpapering platform with no side rails (5:51) Query co-host Shelley demolishing wall with sledgehammer—no PPE (31:42)		Dangling cables (20:11), clutter and lead (20:15) H1: cord on ground, standing over it (40:58)
32	H2: Query use/location of gas cylinder in bedroom (3:45)		H3: Dangling cables/leads (2:45) H3: walkway clutter (6:43) Promotion of "pushed to the edge" and "breaking point" e.g. Harry, Sarah(1:03:08)
33	Query why worker needs to straddle timber and gaps when floor cover could be used (4:24) H4: Demolishing wall—flying debris and dust—no PPE (4:28) H4: Luke has PPE eye wear sitting on cap whilst planing wood with a Makita hand tool—wood chips flying in air—no PPE	H3: Non observance of hardhat sign (3:05; 37:42) H1: no social distancing (11:40, 31:14) Safety sign strewn on ground—perceived as not significant (5:12)	Low dangling power lead (1:37) H5: walkway clutter (1:55) H2: Low power lead (7:36) H1: Low power lead (31:10; 43:34) H3: Low power lead (37:44) H4: cluttered stair entry (38:06)
34	Query use of gas cylinders inside (1:55) e.g. and H1 hallway with leads and clutter (31:42, 37:03) H1: Demolishing walls with no PPE (45:45)	H5: Query Covid social distancing observance	Leads on ground and dangling (1:56-2:00); e.g. H1(28:58)

Episode	Skylarking, Lax PPE Usage/questionable methods/practices	Purported Lax/No PPE Signage/Instruction Observance	Site Appearance: Untidy, clutter, messy, pedestrian obstacles (slip/trip hazards), hygiene
35	Query use of gas cylinders inside e.g. hallway with leads and clutter (1:57)	H5&4: Query Covid social distancing observance (12:32, 37:30)	Leads on ground and dangling (2:19) H4: leads on ground and clutter (36:11) & H5 (49:08))
36		Query compliance with social distancing (49:35)	H5: Hallway clutter (2:19); H4&3: mess and clutter (3:31, 5:36) Site clutter (1:55, 3:47) H1: site clutter (10:19)
37	No PPE—demolishing (2:11; 27:33); e.g. George (H4) using crow bar ladder prying old weather board with no eye protection (45.12)	Query compliance with social distancing (3:45, 17:13)	
38	H1: Adequacy of grabbing/handling insulation without gloves (22:50) H4: Query Luke climbs back into the house and fall and injures his palm, goes to hospital (27.01)		Cluttered/messy sites (1:43) Clutter and low hanging lead along busy thoroughfare (18:45)
39	Site skylarking—dancing around plant and equipment (10:00)	Query compliance with social distancing (39:37)	H4: low hanging leads (40:41)
40	H4: (Macca)—no PPE, nail/screw gun (16:32)	Query compliance with social distancing (2:31); Sarah, "So many people everywhere." Query whether hardhat sign at front (propped against wall) is being observed (H3, 11.21)	H4: dangling leads (8:28) H4: Cluttered/messy site—four workers working under light at night (19:51) H4: clutter, pedestrian obstacles, mess (47:40)

(continued)

Table 6.1 (continued)

Episode	Skylarking, Lax PPE Usage/questionable methods/practices	Purported Lax/No PPE Signage/Instruction Observance	Site Appearance: Untidy, clutter, messy, pedestrian obstacles (slip/trip hazards), hygiene
41	H1: 2 workers using nail/screw power tools but no PPE (6:12)	PPE sign not observed (3:30) H5: Query compliance with social distancing; at least 12 workers surround by mess clutter in one room (28:49)	H5: Dangling power cables (below head height) (9:25)
42	H4: 4 workers in a confined space (bathroom)—no PPE (15:04)	Query 9 workers in one room—Covid distancing protocols (14:18)	
43	H1: using sanding machine in dusty environment with no PPE (17.37) H3: Query placement of 'Jetfire' style gas heater and LPG cylinder in an indoor setting around debris, dust and clutter—not operating (23:18; 45.41). These heaters are LPG-fired and suitable for commercial applications (warehouses and factories and other well-ventilated workplaces). Query blurring of domestic setting, more confined setting having regard to fumes as a consequence of placement in small room with potentially poorer ventilation than large spaces		Clutter in small spaces with several workers (26:15) H1: working around dangling cables (48:50) and H3: low hanging cords with 4 workers in close proximity (23:19)

Episode	Skylarking, Lax PPE Usage/questionable methods/practices	Purported Lax/No PPE Signage/Instruction Observance	Site Appearance: Untidy, clutter, messy, pedestrian obstacles (slip/trip hazards), hygiene
44	H1: Query placement of 'Jetfire' style electric heater and LPG cylinder in a small indoor setting near other plant and unsecured cables—space appears small (1:30) H1: Query worker standing on a precarious bucket stacked on another bucket sanding gyprock (8:26)		
45	H4: Luke using fine mist paint spray gun with no PPE (44:10)		
46	H2: Query workers doing a "McDonalds run" (George and Franklin) and Franklin driving work car and eating food between steering wheel—right hand used to eat whilst left is holding on to chips leaning against steering wheel—appears as a potential road distraction (15:45)	PPE sign shoved on side of entry—states PPE MUST BE WORN e.g. hi viz mandatory (9:08), yet at 9:20 Scotty Cam is walking over mesh steel—no Hi Viz and another worker just has a whole T shirt. Query the inconsistency around perceived mandatory enforcement	Low hanging cable—should be hooked (9:42)

(continued)

Table 6.1 (continued)

Episode	Skylarking, Lax PPE Usage/questionable methods/practices	Purported Lax/No PPE Signage/Instruction Observance	Site Appearance: Untidy, clutter, messy, pedestrian obstacles (slip/trip hazards), hygiene
47			H5: Pedestrian worker at night in artificial light—cables in dark strewn around clutter on ground in small space (2:31); and general clutter (32:43) H1: Cluttered narrow walkway (6:08) H4: cluttered/messy small areas—several workers (9:49)

Episode	Skylarking, Lax PPE Usage/questionable methods/practices	Purported Lax/No PPE Signage/Instruction Observance	Site Appearance: Untidy, clutter, messy, pedestrian obstacles (slip/trip hazards), hygiene
48	H2: George being silly skylarking on step ladder blowing drying his hair dancing (7:47) and worker doing "moon" walk with outdoor blower on his face (8:19) H4: Concerning scene where Jasmin loses an inadequately secured coffee table and chair in the middle of the road (she was assisted by store staff to load it using rope); "Box fell off…onto highway" (11:20). Inadequate system of secure packing—matter trivialised (12:51); "Box fly off the back of the car because you have given me a Ute" (13:22) H1: Tilers cutting tiles using bench wet circular saw—no apparent PPE (16:48); dust from a handheld power tool (16:52); cutting under pressure(17:15) H4: Worker on ladder using nail gun—no PPE (21:37); no eye protection (22:51); lax use of respiratory PPE around work dust (23:02) H1: Query—When Harry (non trades qualified) starts cutting tiles without full PPE; no capturing hoods; generally same for other houses as workers scramble before tools down (23:58-24:30)	No social distancing as "hordes of hungry workers" queue for pizzas (20:21)	H1: Clutter, several workers (15:20)

(continued)

Table 6.1 (continued)

Episode	Skylarking, Lax PPE Usage/questionable methods/practices	Purported Lax/No PPE Signage/Instruction Observance	Site Appearance: Untidy, clutter, messy, pedestrian obstacles (slip/trip hazards), hygiene
49–50 Total Instances	No work performed (auction) 70	No work performed 30	No work performed 75

substantiated. Rather, the fact fans have not only turned to social media but to the authorities is indicative of a potentially systemic and unresolved issue at this workplace (Brennan, 2023).

Figure 6.3 presents the number of instances of behaviours and attitudes collectively described as intangible, given the level of subjectivity attached to them. Figure 6.4 presents the average per episode of possible events. They are described as intangible hazards because of the non-physicality of these events. That is alcohol depiction, gender stereotyping and the occurrence of potential psychosocial harm are not as evident[21] as actions that are more tangible such as spray painting without a respiratory mask.[22] Of significance to this study is that these behaviours support recent developments by regulators in Australia for the need to expressly address exposure to such risks.[23] In other words, a workplace culture that tolerates questionable gendered language or jokes, aggression, bullying, fatigue, alcohol normalisation may potentially expose individuals to harm.[24]

PORTRAYAL OF ALCOHOL AT WORK

Research generally suggests an association between permissive alcohol use or tolerance and a workplace climate with potentially lower workplace safety (Roche et al., 2009). To date, little research has examined the relationship between workplace drinking culture and alcohol consumption patterns among construction workers. Exploring the sociological role alcohol plays in any workplace highlights the importance of focusing on safety and strengthening the culture of workplace safety. It is posited knowledge of how such risks extend to the safety of co-workers and the wider workplace environment is likely to have a greater impact than a narrow focus on the drinking habits of an individual per se where interventions could be targeted to assist that individual. Alcohol is featured on The Block in the form of product placement and consumption. Alcohol was consumed, or appeared to be consumed both in social settings, that

---

[21] In E19–20, 32 references to working late at night, time pressures and fatigue were made but were not readily measurable.

[22] E11: House 2 (18:17).

[23] See amendments to the *Work Health and Safety Regulation 2011 (Qld)* effective 1 April 2023.

[24] See *Model Managing psychosocial hazards at work* Code of Practice (2022), SafeWork Australia.

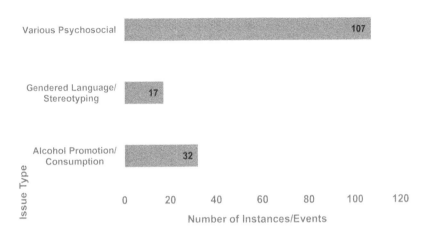

Fig. 6.3 Intangible issues—48 episodes where work was conducted

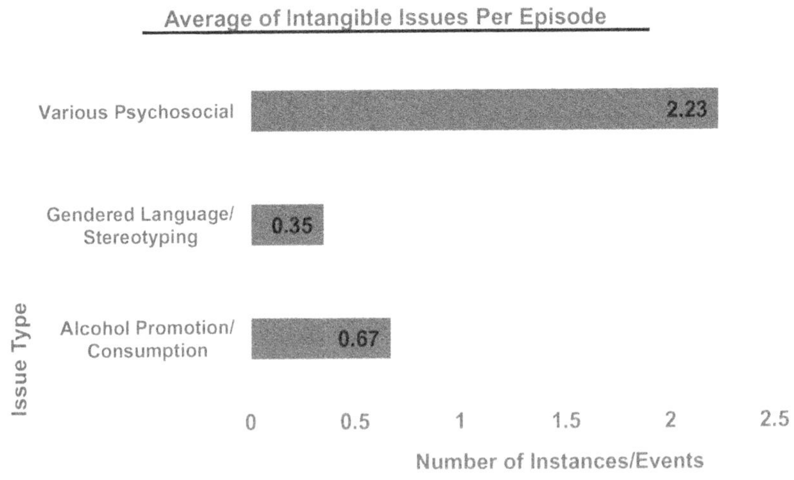

Fig. 6.4 Intangible issues—averaged per episode (48 episodes where work was conducted)

is after work drinks (post "tools down") and in circumstances where it was unclear to the viewer whether work had ceased. That is, contestants could be up all hours preparing for a room reveal, and it was not actually clear when work ceased. Tools down may be a reference to power tools but the show was explicit in its portrayal of couples working all hours of the night (refer to Table 6.2).

The nature of the content observed concerning alcohol was actual use (consumption) or implied use (promotion of brands and product placement). Observations for patterns of alcohol tolerance and depiction were limited to the work site only, and there is no suggestion workers were observed to be adversely affected by alcohol at work on The Block. The deterrent aspect of alcohol consumption due to its effects has culminated in workplace policies where alcohol is not universally condoned because of the risk arising out of a hazard by an individual under the influence of a stupefying substance. On the other hand, alcohol is the most abused substance in the world and its regular use is socially and culturally tolerated (Savic et al., 2016). Thus, workers' perceptions of alcohol availability, awareness of colleagues' alcohol consumption at work (descriptive norms) and peer approval of alcohol consumption (injunctive norms) could potentially encourage risky drinking behaviours. This is because the construction industry, with traditional group norms and mateship culture, may foster a workplace climate where alcohol is easily accessible and acceptable (Roche et al., 2020).

Research surrounding the effects of alcohol at construction sites suggests the need to implement policies and strategies to minimise the likelihood of harm caused by alcohol consumption (Roche et al., 2020). Sawicki and Szóstak (2020) examined 219 accident reports and found 17.4% of incidents indicated alcohol as a contributing factor. The authors identified that the presence of alcohol onsite as evidenced by empty beer cans in the litter piles (2020: 24) adversely impacted the environment and recommended a need for strict alcohol-free site compliance. Pidd et al. (2006) observe construction workers appear to have the propensity to underestimate risks associated with drinking, or not heed safety precautions and protective equipment on site, and thus engage in behaviours that might be risky to their HSW. That alcohol consumption at a construction worksite should not be tolerated is obvious. Workers affected by alcohol around moving items of plant and machinery along with pedestrian traffic could potentially result in risk of injury or death (Sawicki & Szóstak, 2020). Thus, the literature on workplace HSW considerations must outweigh approval of personal use of alcohol at work on construction sites (Roche et al., 2020).

Yet alcohol norms found in this research were more likely to be consistent with a culture of drinking than one that prohibits alcohol at a construction site. Alcohol-related imagery is featured 32 times or on average, nearly two times every three episodes in the form of product placement and purported consumption.[25] The show appeared to promote an environment in which workers' alcohol consumption patterns were normalised. A clear example of trivialising alcohol on the show was a worker walking around a cluttered and busy site with a glass bottle of what appeared to be Corona beer in his hand whilst construction was being conducted.[26] Workers' perceptions of alcohol availability, awareness of colleagues' alcohol consumption at work and peer approval of alcohol consumption in the form of group drinking were overt. Yet this behaviour is at odds with traditional blue collar workplace policy where alcohol availability is controlled and generally discouraged so as to reduce consumption and increase awareness of alcohol-related risks to workplace safety. There appeared to be no positive attempt to consider cultural norms regarding the social unacceptability of drinking within the workplace (Safe Work Australia, 2023).

Consumption and promotion of alcohol on The Block acted as a form of socially acceptable behaviour. The casual approach taken by contestants to alcohol and trivial regard to when and where alcohol was consumed at the site reinforced a perception of a socially acceptable drinking culture at work. Workplace culture plays a particularly important role in shaping emerging alcohol consumption patterns (Roche et al., 2020). Normalising alcohol at work suggests a socialisation process whereby workers adopted such customs in order to belong as a form of collective conscience. Sanctioning alcohol consumption as acceptable conduct on the show signalled to viewers that workplace rules, values, and norms concerning alcohol use were liberal, casual or ambiguous. This is another example of dissonance through trivialisation. This attitude could create a skewed view between management's requirement for stringent control of workers affected by alcohol during work hours and pressure to tolerate

---

[25] Refer to supplementary data for types and nature of depiction.
[26] E37 at H1 (49:41).

or condone workplace norms for alcohol use at work-related social or celebration events that are important for team and morale building.

It is argued the alcohol-related culture of the wider work organisation predominately shapes drinking behaviour. On The Block, there was a perception that it was acceptable to have alcohol present at the workplace and consume alcohol after tools down or after hours. On various occasions, contestant workers consumed alcohol whilst still in PPE.[27] It is therefore arguable that as they were still at the construction site and in PPE, then they have not technically downed tools (the colloquial term used to cease work by the presenter Cam Scott). For example, in E39 (at 5:10), Tam (H5) was filmed returning from an event as a front seat passenger holding on to a glass of champagne as if to suggest "one for the road or traveller".[28] Whilst there appears to be no specific law preventing Victorian road passengers from drinking alcohol in a vehicle pursuant to the relevant legislation, the Victorian government does advise that passengers do not engage in drinking because alcohol-affected passengers "could distract a driver".[29] This observation is made to support the normalisation of the alcohol argument as a workplace continuum. That is, Tammy returned home and resumed painting the interior of the room into the evening after the celebration. Yet prior to entering the passenger side of the vehicle, Tammy and her winning team mates were enjoying what appeared to be a bottle of Verve Cliquot Champagne. The viewer is entitled to query why work would need to commence after celebratory drinks. This appeared to be a split shift because work resumed after the event.

The Block supports the argument alcohol consumption plays a complex role in Western society in that it is valued as a socially and culturally accepted form of behaviour, and conversely, it is viewed as a social and health risk (Chrzan, 2012). At workplaces where alcohol was discouraged, consumption of alcohol was lower than at worksites where alcohol consumption was accepted, encouraged and liberally tolerated (Thorisen et al., 2022). On The Block alcohol was not discouraged and was consumed both in social settings, that is work drinks and in

---

[27] See E37 or E43.

[28] Australian colloquial expressions used often by tradesmen.

[29] *Road Safety Act 1986* or Road Management Act 2004. Vic Roads (2020) https://www.vicroads.vic.gov.au/safety-and-road-rules/driver-safety/drugs-and-alcohol/alcohol-and-road-safety#:~:text=This%20is%20an%20offence%20even,passengers%20could%20distract%20a%20driver.

circumstances where it was unclear to the viewer whether work had ceased. This observation is based on the fact that contestants were sitting at the site surrounded by plant and equipment still wearing Hi-Viz protective clothing and consuming alcohol onsite (or purported to be doing so). Furthermore, as the lines on the program continued to blur with increasing pressure to complete rooms sometimes minutes before a room reveal, the viewer was left confused about the delineation between home and work life, and when work actually ceased, and when alcohol actually stopped being consumed. This blurring of drinking and work patterns suggests co-worker behaviour and expectations about the use of alcohol are causally connected to employees' consumption patterns, and that alcohol-related workplace cultural norms influence workers' drinking behaviours and styles (Chrzan, 2012).

Perceptions concerning alcohol normalisation at work have been the subject of public scrutiny. For example, alcohol product placement at the worksite has been identified as a questionable practice by authorities. In the UK, Carlsberg was admonished for delivering a large crate of beer to workers at a building site (Arther, 2016). Despite Carlsberg insisting that no alcohol was consumed onsite, the UK's Advertising Standards Authority upheld the decision because alcohol was linked with the worksite despite the fact no alcohol was consumed. The link between alcohol and potentially dangerous machinery in the work environment was regarded as contextually problematic. Table 6.2 provides examples where alcohol placement was conspicuous on The Block. This supports the observation alcohol was something considered to be at the lower end of risk concern. In other words, it was tolerated and regarded as a low cultural risk in a normative sense. That is unless someone actually sustained injury from alcohol consumption, then alcohol, responsibly, can be culturally tolerated.

From this perspective, workplace culture concerning alcohol could be more responsibly shaped on the show by developing workplace norms regarding alcohol use in circumstances where its depiction is omitted during instances of actual work. Otherwise, the risk perception is seen as low because condoning its use at work is essentially encouraging the development of risky alcohol-related norms. Depiction should be limited to celebratory events such as the auctions (Episodes 49–50); or offsite where the workers might responsibly consume alcohol to promote the development of low-risk alcohol-related norms. But the lines between socialisation, work and alcohol blurred. By facilitating and supporting norms that promote responsible alcohol use at the workplace, the presentation of alcohol in a trivial manner could be avoided.

Gendered Language and Attribute Stereotype Description and Communication: "Words, Words, Words"—Matter; Don't They?[30]

The use of questionable language or gestures on The Block which appeared to perpetuate gender stereotypes including peculiar words to describe people, was observed on occasion. On the one hand, some of these expressions may have appeared inconsequential or harmless, but on the other, their use in contemporary settings may also appear antiquated and pointless. Observations revealed on some 17 occasions, questionable words and phrases were applied. When do gratuitous comments or metaphors become inappropriate (Kittay, 1988) at the workplace, and at what point does language become discriminatory? In the 23rd minute of the first episode, the affable show host Cam Scott with 30 years experience on the tools as a "chippie",[31] referred to one derelict house as "old girls" who "will come up a treat" to describe recycled buildings and materials[32] Is this a slur on elderly women as abandoned objects capable of being tidied up to look presentable, or just casual acceptable workplace communication? Did Jade mean to say "she's a bit old and a bit haggard" to describe the discarded light fitting capable of being revived to thing of beauty in H3?[33] Furthermore, in E37 "old girls" was referenced to "huge amount of Botox" to describe the faces of the properties. The language in these contexts suggested a form of benevolent sexism guided by physical artefacts legitimised through traditions (Meagher, 2017). But as suggested above, construction work is contained in a male-dominated industry and the use of signs, gestures, and language

---

[30] This sub-title was inspired by Shakespeare's Hamlet (A2S2: 192), William Shakespeare. Shakespeare Navigators. 1603. http://www.shakespeare-navigators.com/hamlet/H22.html#192.

[31] A colloquial Australian term for carpenter.

[32] E1: 23:15.

[33] E3: 27:41.

can have the unintended consequence of being construed as patriarchal within a monocultural, that is male-based universe. Engendering inanimate objects such as building materials can therefore have ideological consequences because of the application of human features being either feminine or masculine (Meagher, 2017).

The use of gendered language at work is not necessary (EIGE, 2023), and is especially irrelevant when a man of influence in a male-dominated industry has described how derelict dwellings will be transformed into a thing of beauty and desire which eventually will be sold to the highest bidder. The houses appeared to be portrayed as a "woman" who can be controlled and her fate will be decided by the controllers. Why must the show engender these houses? Objects referred to as gendered items and tolerance of such language usage perhaps reflect a larger issue at the worksite; namely, attitudes about appropriate communication are cognitively trivialised.

The normalisation of unusual or pointless communication on The Block at times was re-enforced by those in positions of power. It is contended that such language has the unforeseen consequence of being construed as discriminatory because the meaningless application of terms perpetuates stereotypes and trivialises respectful communication at the workplace. This observation is not concerned with cancelling conversations at the workplace, but at what point does language become redundant or even discriminatory? "Knucklehead"[34] is a form of slang used to describe persons who possess a risky mentality, have little or no regard to one's health and wellbeing and generally people who do not think straight (Muñoz-Laboy et al., 2012). It is a derogatory term in that a "knucklehead approach" is myopic in nature (Muñoz-Laboy et al., 2012). The Cambridge dictionary (2023) defines a knucklehead as a stupid person.

It may be that the presenter was being trivial because he is an affable former chippie (carpenter), but it is arguable that the use of such a term could be misconstrued. Whilst it is doubtful Cam Scott's regular use of the word Blockheads was made in a malevolent fashion, it should be noted Blockhead is synonymous with describing someone as stupid in the

---

[34] E34.

same context that knuckleheads are dumb, risk takers. It is likely being used as a term of endearment because of its nexus to the show's title. But despite the play on words, the term Blockhead is potentially offensive when used as a cognate with the knucklehead definition (Cambridge, 2023, Macmillan, 2023).[35] For example, one would not cavil with a nickname such as Blockstar or Blockster etcetera. Again, the observation is made in the spirit of enquiry.

Indeed, the context of some of the language and gestures on The Block perpetuated well-known gender stereotypes beyond the feminine-animate object nexus, but were deemed inconsequential. When do gratuitous comments or mimicked sounds and gestures become inappropriate (Rosen & Shoenberger, 2021) at the workplace; and at what point does communication become unnecessary or discriminatory? In E6 the sound-effect of a wolf whistle might seem incidental or meaningless on its own. But it was raised in the context of Luke (H4) being a model, and leg waxing and his personal attributes generally. The depictions were very light-hearted, but it does reinforce the need to be mindful of context in communication. It should be noted that in Victoria, where the show is filmed, wolf whistling is likely to be considered an act of sex discrimination at work and could attract regulatory action pursuant to the *Fair Work Act 2009*. The wolf whistle was mimicked yet its intention is open to interpretation.

Irrespective of intention, the tolerance of antiquated language for attributable features re-enforces and perpetuates stereotypes or at the very least, trivialises language to the point that what is being said is inconsequential. Despite the ambiguity of gratuitous comments on the show, recent regulatory amendments to psychosocial hazards suggest trivialisation of engendered language should not be encouraged. In a traditionally masculine industry such as construction work, these issues may seem irrelevant when one considers some of the life-threatening, high-risk work activities being undertaken. However appropriate communication and consultation are matters of compliance. This is because workplaces that tolerate untoward communication, even in jest, could attract regulatory

---

[35] https://www.macmillandictionary.com/dictionary/british/blockhead.

attention.[36] When stereotypes are re-enforced at work, trivialisation of certain words and gestures would likely be considered as an unresolved socio-cultural HSW issue.

Various Psychosocial Hazards

In the *Prince* (2019) decision, the Commission accepted the injured worker felt harassed and bullied during the filming of *House Rules*. It was accepted that conflict and tension at the workplace were encouraged. Applying the list of common psychosocial hazards identified in the *Code of Practice* (2022) for managing psychosocial hazards at work, a spectrum of potential hazards on The Block was observed to suggest a poor psychological environment. These included observations concerning unrealistic job demands, low job control, poor emotional support and unclear role clarity. The work climate produced visible displays of fatigue, aggression and interpersonal conflict.

It was observed there were up to potentially 107 occurrences of questionable conduct and psychosocial events in this tele-real drama. The number is not the point because some depictions are open to interpretation, however, it is not known to what extent participants on The Block were inducted in terms of workplace culture, respect for human rights, anti-discrimination policies, and protocols around bullying and harassment. It was evident the spectacle is premised on winning significant prize money, and creating a dramatic atmosphere of tension as each couple attempted to outperform one other at room reveals. In this context, it is not known to what extent psychosocial hazards have been adequately considered. In light of the fact producers in 2023 explained the show has "needed a bit of psychological warfare" (Haigh, 2023), it is less likely any significant attempts were made to comprehensively mitigate the risk of psychosocial harm in Season 16. Psychosocial hazards are defined as those aspects of work design and the organisation and management of work, and their social and environmental contexts, which have the potential to cause psychological, social or physical harm (Kirsten, 2022: 5).

---

[36] E6: 17:41, E28: 5:45, E46: 36:47.

Aggression

Consider the extraordinary scenes during widely reported and so-called "Hell Week". In E33–35 the teams were expected to plaster hundreds of square metres of walls of Gyprock, paint and flooring materials and light installations. The footage revealed chaotic, cramped and crowded work conditions which appeared at odds with building recommendations during the pandemic around social distancing. The number of workers at the site was significant (see the timelapse scene at E33:37:10). As an aside whether or not the best practice for working in or around pedestrian traffic was observed during the height of the global pandemic may be open to conjecture. (This atmosphere was aptly described as being hellish.) But there can be no doubt toxic workplace interactions took place in E33. Given the level of hectic activity on the day, or "chaos" as described by Scott Cam, it is fair to speculate that the environmental conditions may have been a proximate causative factor for antisocial workplace behaviour in the following vignette at E33: 37:15-:

Scott Cam (SC):	*Out the front there is steady stream of deliveries and it's chaos.*
Sarah (S) (H4):	*I was just standing outside our house and kind of witnessed H4's plasters come pick up a board of plaster and take it.*
SC:	*Having just witnessed Luke's plasterers stealing their gyprock. Sarah gets on the phone to George*
S:	*You know that plaster out the front of our house, that's ours yeah. I am about to go guns blazing and I need that confirmation. So got my big girls pants on and went into H4…my plaster sheet was just about to be hung on a wall and I need that back so I went straight to the plasterers. Um guys you know that sheet you just took from the front, we actually need that. Is there anyway you can get that back to me?*
Plaster (P):	*Nah*
S:	*That's mine that you've just taken.*
P:	*[Censored] on the ground mate*
S:	*The reaction from the plasterer wasn't the greatest. He basically lost it and was using all sorts of profanities.*

	Sarah then proceeds to explain what occurred to her building team about being sworn at.
S:	That was quite aggressive. That way that he spoke. It's hard when I have to deal with it because George isn't here. I don't like confrontation. Horrible as a woman. That's the way that person speaks to you…I didn't have George onsite.
	Sarah is very visibly upset and cries about the confrontation.
Luke (L from H4):	Yeah so there was a bit of an altercation between Sarah and my plaster. Sarah was not happy.
	Sarah's builder and Sarah then enter H4
Jasmin:	But you were a bit feisty. You didn't deserve to be sworn at. If you gonna march up and sort of be like that. You don't deserve it but that's kind of communication on a tradies' site unfortunately.
	The matter is escalated to Supervisor Dan for investigation.
SC:	This kind of behaviour is not appropriate so Foreman Dan steps in.
S:	I am crying because I am angry. Plasterer is yelling me at me for no reason
	Supervisor Dan concludes there was a bit disrespect and Luke undertakes to reprimand the plasterers.
S:	I learnt very quickly you have to stand up for yourself especially on a job site.
George (G):	Job sites are quite rough they are quite frantic.

This scene can be described as confrontational and a legitimate example of workplace conflict. It was evident that Sarah, a schoolteacher, was negatively affected. The scene was concerning because it demonstrated several misconceptions about workplace behaviour. By acknowledging rough (swearing) language or aggressive behaviour, a workplace should take appropriate action rather than accepting this as the status quo (see Jasmin's attitude below). Allowing Luke (J4) to reprimand the offender rather than appointed supervisors taking action is also a demonstration that the incident was not properly addressed.

Foul language and disrespect are not to be tolerated at any workplace according to Australia's Model Code of Practice on managing psychosocial hazards at work psychosocial hazards workplace and aggressive behaviour include yelling. Furthermore, poor workplace relationships or interpersonal conflict are potential workplace hazards. The demonstration of this heated disagreement and the disparaging and rude comments that followed is a good example of psychosocial risk. But the way in which the matter was concluded was trivialised to some extent because the scene was highly emotive and as explained by the narrator, it was chaotic. It was not demonstrative of management's commitment to ensure effective consultation. It did not appear that the concerns about psychosocial health and safety were taken adequately and the viewer was left wondering if this was just the norm where men dominate construction sites. At the risk of sounding Pollyanna about appropriate language on construction sites, both Sarah and Jasmin alluded to a certain status quo. Sarah implied she had to adopt an alpha male role and "man it out" (as was the phrase used by her husband when he injured his hand) because her husband was not on site and she had to confront this male on her own. Jasmin concluded this is what occurs on a construction site. This evidence supports the research that the construction industry is "known to be highly masculinised" which has the consequences of "work practices detrimental to employees' wellbeing" (Galea et al., 2022). These authors make a correlation between job demands and aggressive and sarcastic language. These ingredients combined with time pressure led to peer harassment and otherwise unpleasant or toxic behaviour (Galea et al., 2022).

The failure in this scene was that it presented a useful opportunity for the producers to intervene rather than simply allow Luke to take action. He was not the manager. There should have been a proactive rather than reactive approach from management. In other words, the content could have been an example of addressing a workplace issue with appropriate intervention. This scene matters beyond the altercation as the stark reality is that construction sites are toxic and unacceptable for many women. Gerber (2022) correctly argues that:

> *Women don't want to work in macho environments where they feel they don't belong. To attract women, the culture has to change to become less 'blokey', less aggressive, more diverse and more inclusive. But it's a classic Catch-22 situation – women don't want to work in a toxic culture, and the culture won't change without more women.*

Jasmin and Sarah unfortunately accepted their lot at the workplace. Toxic attitudes on construction sites are universal and in the US, women have reported barriers to entry including hostility at the construction site, belittling, harassment, fear of physical assaults and actual assault (NYCOSH, 2024).

Stress and Antagonism: *Dirty Rotten Mongrel*

Episode 33 also depicted a distraught and distressed Harry as he was "pushed too far". Against this backdrop, Harry was agitated because he perceived unfair distribution of workload (that is he had to restore his old door whilst others got new doors). Harry who already had been portrayed as someone less trustworthy than Jimmy (H5) was confronted by Foreperson Keith who suspected Harry was trying to gain an unfair advantage by performing works not permitted at a certain stage. A confrontation ensued, and it was clear the scene was made for dramatic viewing as the exchanges became heated. The scene depicted Harry exclaiming he was "pissed off". The perception that Harry was a sneak, "doesn't like being caught out" and "every time I turn around, he's doing something wrong" were examples of creating drama, obviously, but they were also an illustration of cultivating a toxic workplace atmosphere. This is because Harry has been depicted as being inexperienced, disorganised and deceptive at work (there were several tense scenes in E26–27 between Harry and supervisors Keith or Dan). This aspect of the construction site dynamic was dramatised as a boxing ring contest against Keith and Harry with each party winning rounds in the fight. The drama of course continued when a supervisor explained to the popular couple, Jimmy and Tam that Harry engaged in unauthorised activities. Harry the rule breaker was once again vilified and Jimmy quipped "There's the Block rules and Harry's rules and that's why Keith and Dan spend most of their time up there at House 1".[37]

The portrayal of Harry (H1) as a dirty, sneak and cheat was a common season theme.[38] This type of characterisation (Kavka, 2012) was promoted throughout the show to incite tension between Harry and other contestants. In the case of *Prince* (2019) it was found there was

---

[37] E33: 49:19.
[38] E17, 29–30, 33.

"little doubt" the worker was placed in a hostile and adversarial environment in the course of her employment with Seven. Prince was perceived she was hated as producers encouraged her to be critical of other teams' work and was vilified. Comparably Dirty Harry was viewed as "shady" whilst the hardworking Jimmy at H5 was cast as a worker who extolled the virtue of playing by the rules.[39] In several scenes, Harry appeared clearly distressed at the worksite. This is because Harry (H1) technically trespassed during lockdown (see E18) and was exposed for breaching what was supposed to be lockdown protocol. That is whilst local authorised persons were deemed essential workers and therefore permitted to work onsite, the contestants opted to return to their respective states due to border closures. Harry lived nearby and was caught returning to site without permission. In light of the directions issued by the Victorian government, it is doubtful Harry's trespass was a reality TV invention for drama. It is more likely than not that lack of protocol enforcement on the part of the PCBUs or awareness on the part of Harry provided for great entertainment. From this point onwards, Harry was dubbed Dirty Harry, and this faux-villainous narrative continued throughout the show, stereotyping him as someone not to be trusted. The reality was, however, Harry trivialised strict COVID-19 rules. The cultivation of dysfunction and conflict appeared to create an atmosphere for passive aggression to promote or "foster" Harry, "bad day overreactions" (Overton & Lowry, 2013).

Fat Shaming

In E18[40] viewers were exposed to an awkward incident that attracted online and print media attention (Buaya, 2020; Mastroianni, 2020). Supervisor Keith (K), was called by Daniel (D) from H3 and Builder Ant (A) about a bathroom sub-floor inspection:

K: *Are you after a floor inspection?*
D: *Just before we go too far, we just wanna find out with a bit of a pre-check to see if you are happy with it or not.*

---

[39] E42–43.
[40] At 12:20–13:40.

K: *[scanning the floor] ahm...bit premature yet innit? This isn't really ready for inspection yet. I need everything in place so I can actually see it.*
A: *Right I do have a couple of blocks to which I put in under here.*
K: *[Staring at Daniel] Hey mate have you put a bit of weight on?*

Daniel was clearly unimpressed by Keith's comments (based on his facial expressions and overall body language); and presumably swore after the (censored) weight gain remark. Daniel found himself having to explain his weight to Keith and provide reasons and excuses for any perceived weight gain issues raised by the supervisor. The host and narrator of the show Cam Cox then provided some context to the scene when Daniel had celebrated some weight loss pre-Covid lockdown while chiming in with, "After weeks of lock down this is a problem most of Australia can identify with...but that's not helping Daniel feel any better about it".

At the debrief with his wife, Daniel explained to the producer:

D: *I was like what (emphasised). What are you on about?...It just bugged [censored] It just got under my skin straight away.*
The producer at the end of the scene asked, 'Did you want to say anything like that back? Daniel said, 'nah'.

Later at the construction site, Ant reflected on the "How's the put on weight comment?".

Fat shaming is an identifiable psychosocial hazard and is defined as the act of stigmatising, teasing and otherwise shaming an individual with regard to body size (Fathi, 2011; Spratt, 2021). The portrayal of negative body image (Kinnally & Vonderen, 2014), is a form of targeted discrimination. It exploits an individual's mental and physical state which manifests into a culture of fat shaming by exposing a purported weakness on the part of the victim. It should in all respects be regarded as an example of negative workplace behaviour in that an individual's personal attributes and overall appearance are being assessed.

Body image as a psychosocial hazard can also be a trigger for bullying in the workplace. In Bastoni v ORC International (2019) a worker used humour which amounted to insulting, cruel and demeaning comments about a colleague's weight. The worker saw no harm in telling her supervisor that the supervisor did not feel the cold because she carried "extra padding" [par.10] and that "she felt the Complainant would see the humour in her comments and did not intend to shame her [par.11]. The Commission concluded at [par.61]:

> There was no need to resort to insulting, cruel and demeaning comments when seeking to have the heating in the workplace turned on...They were completely disrespectful and are in no way acceptable.

This case is interesting because the offender deemed her words to be "euphemistic instead of demeaning" [64] and the Commissioner viewed "euphemism simply involves the substitution of roundabout or vague language for that which is harsh or blunt" [par.64]. Discussions surrounding body image are well documented in popular cultural studies and the negative impacts have been examined in reality TV studies. However it is seldom discussed in the context of the workplace and how body image issues can impact health and wellbeing. Fat shaming is commonly defined as the act of stigmatising, teasing and otherwise shaming an individual with regard to body size (Fathi, 2011; Rinaldi et al., 2020; Spratt, 2021). It is a form of targeted discrimination in terms of an individual's mental and physical state which manifests into a culture of fat shaming by exposing a purported weakness on the part of the victim. It should in all respects be regarded as an example of negative workplace behaviour in that an individual's personal attributes and overall appearance are being assessed. Fat shaming might typically include perceptions of laziness, weakness and inability in social settings (Spratt, 2021).

Negative body image has been linked to increased likelihood of psychological distress and eating disorders and to this end, employees' health and performance at work can be negatively impacted by their body image. In addition to potential low morale, absenteeism and poor performance due to mental health issues, body image can also be a trigger for bullying and discrimination in the workplace. Words do matter at work notwithstanding there may have not been any direct intent. It is important to emphasise an objective of workplace harassment and bullying policy and procedure is to be mindful of fellow workers at a macrolevel as some workers may view matters as a violation of basic dignity, courtesy and respect regardless of whether anything was meant by it.

As recent legislative amendments to industrial laws protecting workers' mental health and wellbeing insist on proactive action to minimise the potential for discriminatory conduct it is surprising that the show would not only permit the airing of a reference to a person's weight, but trivialise this reference to an attribute. In the past, body image may have been viewed as a lightweight issue, outside the scope of wellbeing in the workplace. However, it now clearly merits more serious consideration by employers and certainly inclusion in a wellbeing strategy. This is because the culture in which people work determines workplace normativity.

Fat or Lazy?

Questions about construction worker body type are vexed. It seems references to body images or habits such as laziness at a workplace operate to institutionalise the neuro-normativity of unacceptable psychosocial behaviour and reinforce gendered attitudes and beliefs. Fat shaming might also include perceptions of laziness, weakness and inability in a setting (Spratt, 2021). Remarks by supervisors about laziness in several episodes[41] were tolerated by producers who were responsible for the worksite. In addition to the attention brought to Daniel's weight, the camera would often zoom in on George who, by his own admission, enjoyed food. A fair inference that may be drawn by the viewer is that fat shaming is akin to identifying those employees who are presumably lazy. In E4, George (G) and Sarah contract an insulation installer to perform some work on their house. However, this seemingly unremarkable task was met with disappointment and disapproval from both site supervisors Dan and Keith:

> G: *We had so much to do so I got onto HighPages and got an installer to come out and do all the batons underneath. Only cost me two hundred bucks.*
> D: *There's a few lazy people among us.*
> K: *Definitely, like George. He's a sparky, he can fix things. So a hundred bucks an hour to get under the floor and simply either nail or screw some insulation up. Now why isn't George simply doing that himself?*
> D: *Lazy. Very, very lazy.*

---

[41] See E4, 19 and 38.

In response to not having done the insulation themselves, Sarah explained, "So we're going to focus on the painting and execution of the room".[42] It is surprising that two persons in a supervisory capacity would surmise that George's course of action was that of laziness. Could it also be reasonably concluded that the couple quite properly project-managed the task and demonstrated job control? Reference to George's apparent laziness was a common theme in the show and on one occasion, Sarah was visibly distressed and angry about how George had been depicted.[43] Whether or not the agenda was to tolerate "psychological warfare", interacting psychosocial hazards such as low job control and high job demands in addition to name-calling played a role in the workplace.[44]

Fatigue and Wearing It as Badge of Honour

In addition to the interpersonal tension, perhaps the two most common clusters of psychosocial risk concerned fatigue and relational workplace aggression. Tired workers can become angry, upset and emotional, workers as their social tolerance erodes which leads to aggression and abuse (Osgood et al., 2021). These risks are distinct but interconnected because the link between fatigue and suboptimal behavioural performance and workplace conduct is well documented (Wang et al., 2023). On the show, several workers were visibly distressed from lack of sleep, or sleep disturbance and expressed just how tired they were.[45] The show was overt in its promotion of mental exhaustion and explicit in airing aggressive, tense or highly emotive episodes.[46] The episodes were obviously produced for the purposes of entertainment, but in achieving this spectacle, viewers were exposed to sustained inappropriate HSW issues at a construction work site (Galea et al., 2022).

Would The Block fail a Sleep Audit? As set out in Table 6.2, based on remarks made by the participants and combined with visibly tired individuals, the viewer was given the impression sleep was less than 7–9

---

[42] At 17:07.
[43] E38: 54:41.
[44] See E4, 19, 38.
[45] E20, 32, 35, 38, 44.
[46] E3, 13, 22, 25, 30–31, 27–28, 33–34, 37–38.

hours a night. This figure is provided because for optimum work performance sleep hygiene is vital for WHSW (Bono & Hill, 2022). Given that the contestants were working around the clock to complete phases and stages of the build, effective time management for including adequate rest would have been difficult to apply on the show. The fact contestant workers were constantly distracted and had to manage and switch several tasks, including participation in quizzes and activities to win more budget money strongly indicated disrupted or inadequate sleep. Good sleep, much like the other primary needs mentioned previously, is not just desirable but essential for proper physical and mental health (Bono & Hill, 2022). Williamson and Feyer (2000) conducted research on moderate sleep deprivation to determine cognitive and motor performance based on variable sleep patterns. The authors found "The overall implications of the results of this study are clear. They show that the effects on performance of moderate periods of being awake cannot be discounted" (2000: 654). The authors also concluded there was a direct correlation between regular sleep patterns and increased levels of wellbeing.

Conversely, when a person is sleep deprived, there is an increased tendency to overreact (Williamson & Feyer, 2000). It is interesting to note that, like other reality TV shows, The Block was an environment where participants were very emotional, heightened, stressed and generally distressed (refer to comments in Table 6.2). According to the Sleep Health Foundation (2024) good hygiene tips include regular sleep, limit on caffeine intake, avoidance of alcohol and obviously, follow a good routine (see also Williamson and Feyer (2000) on the effects legal alcohol consumption (0.05%) has on workers' sleep patterns). On The Block, McCafe played a prominent role in the service of coffee to the workers at the site, and "tools down" essentially was a euphemism for after-work drinks. This idea of having a drink after work was regularly depicted or referenced in the narrative of Season 16. Combined with a hectic work schedule, the trivialisation of good sleep hygiene was evident. This is concerning considering the following passage made by the foundation:

> *Sleep is directly related to workplace health, safety, and well-being. Sleep-deprived employees are more prone to accidents, reduced productivity, and impaired decision-making, jeopardizing workplace safety. Chronic sleep problems can contribute to chronic health issues like heart disease and obesity, affecting employee well-being and increasing healthcare costs for employers. Conversely, workplaces that prioritise sleep-friendly policies, such as flexible*

schedules or designated nap areas, can boost employee morale and performance, reduce absenteeism, and enhance overall health and safety. Promoting healthy sleep habits in the workplace is a win-win for both employees' well-being and a company's productivity and safety.
https://www.sleephealthfoundation.org.au/sleep-categories/workplace-health-safety-wellbeing

A Culture of Stress

The content often contained contestants feeling moody or anxious. Anger and feelings of being bullied by management were highlighted throughout the show. Whilst is accepted that this is likely symptomatic and a core theme in all reality TV where a focus of angry rumination is televised for the audience, it is worth acknowledging that audience viewers have surmised that the show does promote antisocial behaviour. First, consider the fact that 28 complaints were made to the Media watchdog, Australian Communications and Media Authority (AMCA), and that "The majority of the inquiries related to allegations of bullying, harassment and promotion of anti-social behaviour between contestants" (Knox, 2023). A finding is pending but it is worth reflecting on a news article by the same journalist about the 2019 season entitled "The Block 'all a lie' claim 'bullied' contestants where Tess & Luke give an explosive interview accusing Nine show of impacting mental health" (Knox, 2019). The piece centres around the couple "accusing" producers of "bullying" and feelings of portrayed as "lazy". Of concern was the frank comment that Tess stated that her "mental health isn't right…I wasn't OK…it was all a lie". It was also reported that Tess exclaimed "You guys need to stop filming me because I'm not coping right now for mental health reasons'—and they didn't stop filming". The reports squarely centre on how the couple felt they had been bullied throughout the entire show. The producers confirmed a psychologist and support team were available at all times. However, it is not known if the contestants were inducted about psychosocial hazards or whether a psychosocial risk register exists. Stress places significant importance on wellbeing considerations in construction work. It is the key trigger for workplace tension and conflict creation (Galea et al., 2022). When one considers the immense pressure placed on the contestants, the third column provides a sustained narrative about how pivotal stress was in the process (Table 6.2).

Table 6.2 Season 16 (2020) The Block Observation: Code Book for Typologies 4, 5 & 6[47]

Episode	Alcohol portrayal placement/promotion/consumption	Gendered Language/stereotyping	Various Potential Psychosocial
1	Man in Hi-Viz with Absolute Vodka carton entering worksite—workplace perception consideration (32:39) "Tools Down, Knock off beers, grab a beer" (35:58–36:20)	Antiquated metaphorical language by male to symbolise and conceptualise inanimate objects as women: reference to houses by host, "these old girls will come up a treat"—query male mediation identification (23:00) First use of term "Block Heads" by Scott Cam (29:13). Appears to be used innocuously but query if it used in same context as season progresses, i.e. use of alternative phrase "Knuckle Heads" at E34 below	H3: Query Sarah feeling anxious about the mess and descends into frivolous/trivial remarks about being OCD (a mental illness); repeats this narrative in E44 (21:20). Day and night work session (painting), comment by Jimmy 59:38
2	Group conversations with alcohol after power tools curfew (Coopers bottles) (35:03)		Natasha has a meltdown from feeling overwhelmed about room renovation (43:00). Feelings of being overwhelmed, emotional, frustrated and upset are displayed
3		Query "Here's my light, she's a bit old and a bit haggard" (Jade) (27:41)	Dan and George confrontation about alleged theft of materials ("thieving mongrels") (from 22:00) Continuation of promotion of Natasha distressed crying/sobbing (47:27)

[47] In the broader context of entire system of work.

Episode	Alcohol portrayal placement/promotion/consumption	Gendered Language/stereotyping	Various Potential Psychosocial
4	Coopers beer can placed on ledge (5:07)		Name calling—supervisors Dan and Keith label George "lazy" (16:58, 17:07)
5			
6		Luke is asked by the site supervisors Keith and Dan whether he has worked as a model, and general banter about shaving and leg waxing; a wolf whistle is made; prima facie offensive at a workplace (18:08)	Supervisor berating and belittling carpenter Luke about the carpentry ("seriously is" "pathetic and "crap", "done by five year old" (8:15–30) Luke provides unacceptable reasons for working unsafely with angle grinder. Heated argument between supervisor and Luke about not using vacuum during cement cutting. The quarrel was churlish and unnecessary as central issue was Luke was either deliberately or ignorantly non-compliant (43:05)
7		George—*man it out* (22:00)	Luke trivialising lack of sleep due to noise ("super loud") (2:21) Natasha describes stress and time pressures (7:24)

(continued)

Table 6.2 (continued)

Episode	Alcohol portrayal placement/promotion/consumption	Gendered Language/stereotyping	Various Potential Psychosocial
8	Foreperson Keith opens a can of a what purports to be VB (Victorian Bitter) beer for Foreperson Dan as Dan dusts himself off (after a session of cutting tiles with a power tool presumably, as depicted at 18:30. It is also presumed to be an after job completion drink as they toast each other and wish each other a good weekend (19.18). But they are both onsite and both in PPE. Compare this drink scene with Ash and Tam serendipitously enjoying a champagne lunch at a restaurant at 18:17–33. The scenes are in stark contrast as one is onsite and the other, quite properly, is offsite. In terms of alcohol portrayal values, norms and attitudes surrounding alcohol patterns of consumption, the benefits of alcohol as a reward is liberally promoted		Luke and supervisor Keith amend rift (E6), but issue about potential lax safety attitude not acknowledged (6:03) Luke expresses his attitude toward H5 winners; negative undertones (14:00)
9	Onsite BBQ with alcohol consumption—purportedly surrounded by plant and equipment, debris and clutter (29:48)		Inappropriate humour by Supervisor Keith with George ("You have troubles getting it up") (query relevance of erectile dysfunction inference) (17:21) George H2 unloading materials heated dispute with driver; promotion of tension (43:50) H1, "Hissy fit Harry, grumpy" Supervisors teasing re: dispute (46:29)

Episode	Alcohol portrayal placement/promotion/ consumption	Gendered Language/stereotyping	Various Potential Psychosocial
10			
11			H4 Jasmin very distressed/upset—consider whether health and wellbeing check is provided; viewer is not apprised of psychosocial interventions (11:00) H1: Harry agitated, being berated by supervisors for not project managing, painting into the night ("no sleep the next night completely") (44:29)
12			H2 Sarah: visibly distressed and crying "bloody exhausted" (12:39) All working late into night (20:30) H1 Harry still working and top of wardrobe at height all night, and admits to being "anxious" due to workload and timeframes (22:00); H1 Harry injured due to rushing; sprains ankle outside in cluttered site (indicates medical attention) Query work design in the premises (22:30)

(continued)

Table 6.2 (continued)

Episode	Alcohol portrayal placement/promotion/consumption	Gendered Language/stereotyping	Various Potential Psychosocial
13			H1 Harry is bed-bound; confined to organising; Supervisors, cross-armed and condescendingly, state "No different to last 3 or 4 weeks, let's be honest he didn't do too much"—query attitude on part of supervisor (38:00)
14			H4: Confrontational scene between Supervisor Keith and alleged poor workmanship by builder Macca. No consultation to resolve issue; just heightened tension, threats to dismiss and poor communication evident (38:37–30:25)

6 RESULTS AND DISCUSSION 129

Episode	Alcohol portrayal placement/promotion/consumption	Gendered Language/stereotyping	Various Potential Psychosocial
15			Workers bickering, tension between Daniel (H3) and Jimmy (H5), allegation Daniel is a worksite "dobber" (1:25), escalating tension; Daniel expresses: "dick move, disgusting, moron, have a go at him, piss me off", "dog's act" argument ensues, yelling, Jimmy has issue with being "dobbed on" (10:15–14:45) H2: Tiling until 1:30 in morning due to wall installation error. Did "17 hours tiling", and "still going" (22:48 & 35:23) H4: worked through evening, up at 6:45am (5:00)
16	Alcohol consumption surrounded by plant and equipment—purportedly (20:40)	H4: "She's pretty impressive, her curved wall, at her peak" (5:22)	
17	Debrief ("crisis meeting") still in Hi-Viz in the middle of the worksite with alcohol, Foreperson asks "what's happening?" (21:36)		T1: Harry's reputation/character as sneaky/dirty created (59:41)

(continued)

Table 6.2 (continued)

Episode	Alcohol portrayal placement/promotion/consumption	Gendered Language/stereotyping	Various Potential Psychosocial
18			Query Foreman Dan's comment "now you are telling lies" whilst laughing when George (H3) explains he lost weight (5:42) Foremen Keith appears to fat shame Daniel (T3) (12:41, 13:37) "Put a bit of weight on" comment T1: Harry named and shamed for returning to site without permission (15:00). The trespass is exploited and trivialised for TV. Tension was created but no consequence for returning to site (22:57)

Episode	Alcohol portrayal placement/promotion/consumption	Gendered Language/stereotyping	Various Potential Psychosocial
19			H3: George accused of being lazy by foremen (6:15) H4: Jasmin meltdown (to soundtrack of Star Wars (Darth Vader) (19:00) Jade and Jasmin appointment clash conflict; tension exploited, Jade upset "too nice" (23:08) T1 Harry labelled as "villain" (39:22)—term in context is depreciative in nature and augments narrative in which Harry is belittled or insulted. Whilst Dirty Harry in E29 may be a reference to a Clint Eastwood role, it is also suggestive of a morally corrupt person that may be held in contempt T2: "painting to 3am in the morning" (44:43) T2: "painting to 3am in the morning" (44:43) T4&5: special/exclusive alliance/bond formed having dinner T1&2: special/exclusive alliance/bond formed having a laugh; but T3: couple portrayed as loners, working (48:30)

(continued)

Table 6.2 (continued)

Episode	Alcohol portrayal placement/promotion/consumption	Gendered Language/stereotyping	Various Potential Psychosocial
20		H1: Wall built incorrectly. Query whether "Cam Scott needs to unnecessarily quip "can we have a loser buzzer sound? Thank you" (4:24)	H5: finishing at 3:30 in the morning, still working—past 12:35 am (21:05), "long night tonight" (21:10) Luke": "fatigued last night" (49:30)
21	Alcohol promotion and consumption (spirits, beers, wine) in the middle of the worksite (workers in background) (31:15) H3: Query beer bottle placed in middle of worksite amongst clutter (51:36)		
22	H4: Coopers beers on table—reinforcing the worth or value of alcohol (45:16)		H4: Query confrontation. Luke and Jasmin confronted by judge for copying someone else's design idea Query accusation and approach by producers given that use of the design was disclosed prior to commencement of room; gossip ensues (48:00)

Episode	Alcohol portrayal placement/promotion/consumption	Gendered Language/stereotyping	Various Potential Psychosocial
23	Alcohol placement—half consumed beer—query its relevance (48:44)		H4: Feeling deflated—rumours continue, gossip around the "copycat" issue at H4 constantly systematically brought up to gauge reaction from others (25:17, 32:30) Couples discussing "divide" and "tension", comparing and contrasting others; "we are the same breed", "they annoy me" (48:00–50:00); H4: suspicion of copycats continues (59:30)
24			H4: Luke and Jasmin copycat allegations continue—kitchen bench with H3 (1:27, 8:17)
25			Continuation of kitchen bench saga/confrontation (11:07)

(continued)

Table 6.2 (continued)

Episode	Alcohol portrayal placement/promotion/consumption	Gendered Language/stereotyping	Various Potential Psychosocial
26			Jade: "So much pressure" (2:16) Confrontation between Foreman Keith and George (H2) Despite Harry (H1) disobeying, query need for supervisor to accuse Harry for disliking authority; continuation naughty Harry narrative; negative attitude, Keith promoting friction/tension/antagonism—extremely poor communication and no meaningful consultation; pointless workplace dispute because Harry was unnecessarily accused (21:06, 24:45, 25:30–28:00, 55:00). Dramatization of Harry threatening to walk off The Block (55:20)
27	Regular promotion of alcohol—consumed at birthday celebration—reinforcing its cultural significance (47:31)		Harry (H1): "The fight is on": confrontation with supervisors continued; "Round 1 and Round 2" (10:20); escalating tension (11:55); Harry is badgered, clearly distressed—poor communication ends in dispute—designed to cause reaction (33:30–35:45) H1: painting into the night at height (47:54) Harry (H1): "Round 4" confrontation with Keith (49:00)

Episode	Alcohol portrayal placement/promotion/consumption	Gendered Language/stereotyping	Various Potential Psychosocial
28	Constant reminder of alcohol consumption "Not too early for a beer mate" (Daniel H3 at 5:11) (see also 3:30, 18:27, 22:34)	Query: what's the point of a wolf whistle at Harry's head? (5:45)	Harry's distress (H1) described as "massive tanti" (0:30); Trivialising Keith and Harry dispute ("a love story", 0:50) H1: "big night of painting"—Harry painting at height (5:41) Fight'n in Brighton, continuation of "naughty Harry" label; also described as "passive aggressive" (6:20–8:20) Jasmin very distressed whilst driving (in tears) (11:40) Teams working into night (9 p.m.) (21:39) "Dirty Harry overstepped again" (1:07:33)
29		Query repeated description of Harry as "dirty, rotten mongrel" (27:26)	"Dirty Harry "incident (1:20)
30			
31	"Happy hours beers" Luke and Jimmy (43:02)		
32			Sarah (H2): exhausted (7:42) H3: Daniel agitated because perceived he was called a liar by Foreman Dan—confrontational/antagonistic exchange (26:30–28:00) H4: working into the night (42:29) H3: Foreman Keith badgering Daniel about his work quality "rough as guts" (after late night) (8:39) H4: Time pressures to complete large jobs (floor replacement) (13:20–15:00) H4: Tired (16:48)

(continued)

Table 6.2 (continued)

Episode	Alcohol portrayal placement/promotion/consumption	Gendered Language/stereotyping	Various Potential Psychosocial
33	H2: Winners and grinners BBQ with alcohol but workers still in PPE—cannot ascertain if work has stopped for the day/night (28:32)		"Hellway Week" H5: Build up of "pressure", Natasha expresses "having PTSD" (4:54); emphasis on "rigid schedule" (5:17) Issue and dispute with Harry (H1) about door poorly managed/communicated—presumably to get a rise/negative reaction (no consultation) (34:35–36:30, 41:59, "pissed off" "pushed too far" 42:33) Aggression by plasterer towards Sarah (H2) "lost it", swearing—Sarah very upset by altercation—poorly handled—no consequences for disrespectful conduct (38:15–41:10) Constant tension between Keith and Harry promoted (Harry undermined, feels he is unfairly treated; e.g. H5 got to "pack frame out") 43:20–46:45—poor communication/consultation (H1). Harry is "ushed" Keith then presents allegation to H5 and elicits dirty rotten, mongrel Harry" (47:08–48:09). Harry is always "caught out"—Keith targets Harry (48:45). Harry deemed non-follower of rules by Keith and block favourites Jimmy and Tam (H1 49:25); "everyone knows that" about Harry and rules (49:19)

Episode	Alcohol portrayal placement/promotion/ consumption	Gendered Language/stereotyping	Various Potential Psychosocial
34		Use of term of "knuckleheads" (presumably as alternative to "blockheads" to describe participants (12:11, 14:42)	H1: Harry feeling overwhelmed and stressed (4:57, 5:18); feels aggrieved/ treated unfairly—matter not resolved (5:45); sleep deprived; "eventually you crack" (7:54); "Harry still whinging about the door" comment (42:23); Harry's feelings of being treated unfairly bot addressed (44:08)
35	Gathering around fire pit consuming alcohol still in PPE (not clear if finished for the day) (50:00)		H1: Harry tells Keith he went to bed at 3 (am) no concern about fatigue raised (7:09) George stayed up until 3 a.m. (27:55)
36			Luke admits "knackered"—"start on backfoot, flat, stressed" (3:46, 17:19) H2: Tension; heated discussion/ argument "cameras off"—George "two hours sleep in three days" (10:20–13:20, 18:08); emphasis on overnight work (22:37) (H2)

(continued)

Table 6.2 (continued)

Episode	Alcohol portrayal placement/promotion/consumption	Gendered Language/stereotyping	Various Potential Psychosocial
37	Query Jasmin purporting to hold a can of VB beer at worksite meeting in (6:16) H5: Winners are grinners dinner; query alcohol consumption around cluttered site, plant, equipment (22:27) Tam drinking wine—replete with with cement mixer in situ nearby (48:12) H1: Worker walking around busy work site with glass bottle (appears to be Corona beer) (49:41)	Context and inference—query "Returning the faces of these old girls…and that's gonna require a huge amount of Botox" (Scott Cam) (3:00)	Foreman Keith (who knows Jasmin is upset from the previous evening), persistently asks "what's wrong, too much, don't seem happy?" (19:30–20:00) Daniel (H3)—clearly distressed that H2 builder stole/took his LVL timber and complains "why isn't someone doing something about it?" (35:12–36:14). The producers turns his concerns into vignette "Farmer" wants a "fight" (37:22) Continued focus on Harry being overwhelmed and upset (43:56) H1: "chaos, rush, mayhem", pouring concrete. Barrels being tipped over (48:35, 49:10)

Episode	Alcohol portrayal placement/promotion/consumption	Gendered Language/stereotyping	Various Potential Psychosocial
38			Scenes depicting stress, distress, time pressures, anger, teasing (mainly Harry or George), fatigue frustration, "tired and emotional", "drained" and generally scenes appear to be promoting psychosocial hazards (see generally from 3:15, 8:05, 9:35, 17:30, 18:08, 38:30) Further attacks on George by Foreman Dan; "hopeless mate he's been lazy all day", George hears dan is telling others he is lazy, Sarah is angry and upset (22:00, 23:52–25:00); contestants generally berated in this episode by Foreman Dan (54:41)

(continued)

Table 6.2 (continued)

Episode	Alcohol portrayal placement/promotion/consumption	Gendered Language/stereotyping	Various Potential Psychosocial
39	Alcohol consumption theme continued (celebrating a challenge win and Tam travelling with glass of champagne in car (5:10); yet they resume work painting into the evening—after 9:30 (7:18)—reinforcement of alcohol as a consistent theme—normalising it presence and trivialising it. Extended alcohol consumption and promotion in at 11:09 pm—messy, cluttered site, plant, equipment and gas heaters working and dancing whilst drinking alcohol, "pumping"—with background music (likening it to a rave) (9.37–11.09) "How much do you love beer—beer economy is strong on construction sites, how much beer do you think it's worth—a few hundred." Thanking the workers with a "slab" (carton beer) (25:27); maintaining a status quo of construction workers' positive association with alcohol Jasmin dancing around worksite with wine (45:25), more drinking in a group (45:43)	Query finding 10 of the hottest tradies on the block for a photo shoot (41:00). ...getting their kit off...overt sexualisation of male...starting lifting peoples' shirts up or is that inappropriate...money shot sleazing...stud muffin...starting to get a sweat up". Mindless banter and gestures about "hot tradies"	

6 RESULTS AND DISCUSSION   141

Episode	Alcohol portrayal placement/promotion/ consumption	Gendered Language/stereotyping	Various Potential Psychosocial
40		H2: Emphasis on cultural value and that restoration in an aspirational context is conceptualised from male context "And to help restore this old girl back" (Cam Scott, 14:16)	Jasmin: "So stressed out", "prize for the most stressed, Harry" (3:15); "Only had 20 minutes sleep, I didn't get any (George and bricklayer" (15:25) H3: "Some haven't slept" (23:46) H1: "I was manic" (Natasha breaking down), 25:17), "under a lot of stress" (Harry, 25:40)
41	Winners are grinners dinner at worksite: alcohol reinforcement at work site (25:30) Worker, beer bottle in hand dancing around portable scaffolding (40.06)		H1: Natasha very distressed 22:30 H1: Continued antagonism between Harry and foremen, feeling overwhelmed, stressed (34:40). Solution to alleviate Harry's stress was for Foreman Dan and Keith was to take him out for a wine and pub meal (36:00)
42			Ongoing binary narrative about how Jimmy and Tam (H5) (the favourite/ golden couple) "playing by the rules but Luke once again breaking the rules" (Cam Scott, 1:08–1:17)

(continued)

Table 6.2 (continued)

Episode	Alcohol portrayal placement/promotion/consumption	Gendered Language/stereotyping	Various Potential Psychosocial
43			H1 and 5: Ongoing narrative about tension between Harry and Jimmy re: "easier house", tense/hostile exchange, swearing, "for someone like you" (8:42–10:50; 12:15–13:00); encouragement of conflict and gossip (15:21) Luke despite huge migraine during day says he will be painting all night, all tomorrow, so much to do (47:42)
44	H2: Workers in on a break with beer (appears to be Stella stubbie) (19:08) H5: Tam walking around with a wine while workers assemble gym; "strapping in for a big night, hit it hard" (Jimmy) (19:41)		H5: revisiting Jimmy being upset, "sleep deprivation, pressure" (6:14) H3: Sarah's E1 casual remark in jest (again) about being OCD—which is a mental illness (10:00) H1: "Emotions run high when you are tired" (Natasha) (17:35) H1: "Apprentice just hit the wall, exhausting" (17:58) H2: "Gonna be big one"..."long night ahead (Sarah) (19:55) H4: "Absolutely shattered" (Luke, 20:45), Jasmin very upset (23:19)

Episode	Alcohol portrayal placement/promotion/ consumption	Gendered Language/stereotyping	Various Potential Psychosocial
45	H2: Winners and Grinners dinner "pub quiz" with alcohol—reinforcement of alcohol (29:20)		H4: "Stress and pressure", working into the night (Jasmin, 44:50)
46		Dave Franklin pretending to be Greek with a painted mono-brow/unibrow—presumably stereotyping a Greek male—a joke; assumption that this is funny (21:12) Continuation of E39 sexualised narrative. Query "Super sexy tradie" calendar photo shoot, picking the "hottest tradie" replete with wolf whistle—but not Harry—"too old" (36:47)	More promotion of an all night work session (49:00) Luke: "close to nervous breakdown" (49:12)
47		H4: Query form of social construction by saying "Get this old girl straight again" (Luke; 27:32)	H3: Daniel; time constraint pressures—walks away swearing (20:20) H4: "One step away from a nervous breakdown" (Luke swearing (29:07)—query whether Luke is being trivial or in genuine crisis

(continued)

Table 6.2 (continued)

Episode	Alcohol portrayal placement/promotion/consumption	Gendered Language/stereotyping	Various Potential Psychosocial
48	H4&5 Reminder: "Wine fun—lots of beers" (25:27–45)		H1: "One last stoush between Harry and Keith…no arguing" remark (4:50) H1: "All the shifty stuff that has been going on has to stop" (Keith) (17:31); both supervisors antagonising/arguing with Harry (17:41); questioning and disapproving of Harry's character H4: "Working into the early hours" (24:56)
49–50	No work performed	No work performed	No work performed
Total Instances	32	17	107

References

Aboagye-Mino E., & Emuze, F. (2007). *Construction safety through housekeeping: The Hawthorne effect* (pp. 2027–2038). https://journals.uj.ac.za/index.php/JCPMI/article/view/132/122. Taylor & Francis Online.

Adams, N. (2019). Gravitational hazards. in *The core body of knowledge for generalist OHS Professionals*. Australian Institute of Health and Safety.

Advertising Standards Authority. (2017). *(NZ) ASA ruling on Bisley workwear, 17/205.* https://cdn.asa.co.nz/backend/documents/2017/08/10/17205.pdf. Accessed 22 December 2021.

Ajia v TJ & RF Fordham Pty Ltd trading as TRN Group [2020] NSWDC 371.

Arther, R. (2016). *Carlsberg video banned for linking alcohol with building site.* https://www.beveragedaily.com/Article/2016/09/28/Carlsberg-video-banned-for-linking-alcohol-with-building-site. Accessed 17 August 2022.

Australian Building and Construction Commissioner v Construction, Forestry, Maritime, Mining and Energy Union (The DoubleTree Hilton Case) [2021] FCA 1468.

Australian Standard 1319–1994 (AS 1319) Safety signs for the occupational environment Sydney: SAI Global.

Ayres, T. (2013). Warnings, anti-warnings, and pacifiers. *Proceedings of the Human Factors and Ergonomics Society Annual Meeting, 57*(1), 1698–1701.

Bastoni v ORC International (2019) FWC 38.

Bono, T. J., & Hill, P. L. (2022). Sleep quantity and variability during the first semester at university: Implications for well-being and academic performance. *Psychology, Health Medicine, 27*(4), 931–936. https://doi.org/10.1080/13548506.2021.1971724

Brennan, A. (2023). The block: Fans complain about bullying to Australian Communications and Media Authority *The Week-End Australian*, October 2, 2020.

Buaya, A. (2020). It's 2020, are we still commenting on people's weight? Fans of the block are left fuming at foreman Keith Schleiger for his 'fat shaming' comments about contestant Daniel Joyce". https://www.dailymail.co.uk/tvs howbiz/article-8759503/The-Block-fans-left-fuming-foreman-Keith-Schlei gers-fat-shaming-comments.html. Accessed 31 October 2022.

Buchtmann, L. (2021). Food safety it's in your hands—Reported hand washing and hand sanitiser use in Australian adults August 2019 and August 2020. *Environment and Health International, 21*(1), 1–24.

Cambridge Dictionary. (2023). https://dictionary.cambridge.org/dictionary/english/blockhead. Accessed 22 December 2022.

Chrzan, J. (2012). *Alcohol: Social drinking in cultural context*. Routledge.

Code of Practice. (2019). *Managing the work environment and facilities*. NSW Government.

Collins, P. (2024). *Tradie working on the block sues Channel Nine after allegedly being electrocuted on the job*. https://www.dailymail.co.uk/tvshowbiz/article-13205781/The-Block-tradie-sues-Nine-allegedly-electrocuted.html?ico=topics_pagination_desktop

Conzola, V., & Wogalter, M. (2001). Communication–human information processing (C-HIP) approach to warning effectiveness in the workplace. *Journal of Risk Research, 4*, 309–322.

CSQ. (2021). *Women in construction*. https://www.csq.org.au/wp-content/uploads/2021/02/Women-in-Construction-2021.pdf

Dash Cam Owners Australia. (2024). https://www.youtube.com/c/dashcamownersaustralia

Demarco, M. (2023). *The Block's Steph is left crying in pain as she suffers painful injury during bathroom week"* https://www.dailymail.co.uk/tvshowbiz/article-12455509/The-Blocks-Steph-left-crying-pain-suffers-shock-injury.html

Energy Safe Victoria. (2023). *Gas and LPG safety outdoors outdoor appliances should never be used inside*. https://www.esv.vic.gov.au/community-safety/energy-safety-guides/outdoor-safety/gas-and-lpg-safety-outdoors

Duarte, F., Davel, E., Dupuis, J. -P., & Chanlat, J. -F. (2008). Culture and management in Australia: "G'day mate". In *Gestion en Contexte Interculturel: Approches, Problématiques, Pratiques et Plongées*.

European Institute for Gender Equality EIGE. (2023). *Gender sensitive communication*. https://eige.europa.eu/publications/gender-sensitive-communication/challenges/stereotypes/gendering-animate-objects. Accessed 15 March 2023.

Fair Work Act 2009.

Fathi, F. (2011). Why Weight Matters: Addressing Body Shaming in the Social Justice Community. *Columbia Social Work Review,9*(1), 23–36.

Fields, B. (2024). Toughen up mate: The harmful effects of toxic masculinity on Australian men. *The Junction*. https://junctionjournalism.com/2020/11/04/toughen-up-mate-the-harmful-effects-of-toxic-masculinity-on-australian-men/

Flood, R. L., & Jackson, M. C. (1991). *Creative problem solving*. Wiley.

Galea, N., Powell, A., Salignac, F., Chappell, L., & Loosemore, M. (2022). When following the rules is bad for wellbeing: The effects of gendered rules in the Australian Construction industry. *Work, Employment and Society, 36*(1), 119–138. https://doi.org/10.1177/0950017020978914

Gerber, P. (2022). *Women in construction: Smashing down the concrete walls that keep them out*. https://lens.monash.edu/@politics-society/2022/03/07/1384504/women-in-construction-smashing-down-the-concrete-walls-that-keep-them-out

Guertin, L. (2023). *Hamish and Andy 'disgusted' by The block and 'step in' to protect Eliza*. https://au.lifestyle.yahoo.com/hamish-and-andy-disgusted-by-the-block-and-step-in-to-protect-eliza-003232824.html

Gulamhussein, M. A., Li, Y., & Guha, A. (2016). Localized Tetanus in an adult patient: Case report. *Journal of Orthopaedic Case Reports, 6*(4), 100–102. https://doi.org/10.13107/jocr.2250-0685.592

Haigh, J. (2023). *The block exec producer slams viewer complaints: I'm not happy*. https://www.news.com.au/entertainment/tv/reality-tv/the-block-exec-producer-slams-viewer-complaints-im-nothappy/news-story/5c5c612f7ddda73649763d92a6e9a76d

Hamilton-Smith, L. (2016). *DIY injuries on rise amid home renovation TV boom, Brisbane doctors say*. https://www.abc.net.au/news/2016-12-19/diy-disasters-on-rise-amid-renovation-tv-boom/8133204

Health and Safety at Work (Hazardous Substances) Regulations 2017 (New Zealand).

Industry Update. (2024). *Jetfire LPG industrial space heaters; J25A, J33A, J50A, J70A, J90A and J90SA series*. https://www.industryupdate.com.au/products-details/air-conditioning/24303/jetfire-lpg-industrial-space-heaters-j25a-j33a-j50a-j70a

James, M., Chauncey, A., Ogle-Mustafa, C., & Chichester, M. (2023). Determinants of the use of personal protective equipment: A literature review. *Journal of Education, Society, and Behavioural Science, 36*(2), 1–14.

Haslam, R. A., Hide, S. A., Gibb, A. G., Gyi, D. E., Pavitt, T., Atkinson, S., & Duff, A. R. (2005). Contributing factors in construction accidents. *Applied Ergonomics, 36*(4), 401–415. https://doi.org/10.1016/j.apergo.2004.12.002

Karanikas, N., Khan, S., Baker, P., & Pilbeam, C. (2022). Designing safety interventions for specific contexts: Results from a literature review. *Safety Science, 156*, 105906. https://doi.org/10.1016/j.ssci.2022.105906

Kavka, M. (2012). *Reality TV*. Edinburgh University Press.

King, M. (2009). The problem with negligence. *Social Theory and Practice, 35*(4), 577–595.

Kinnally, W., & van Vonderen, K. (2014). Body image and the role of television: Clarifying and modelling the effect of television on body dissatisfaction. *Journal of Creative Communications, 9*(3), 215–233.

Kirsten, W. (2022). The evolution from occupational health to healthy workplaces. *American Journal of Lifestyle Medicine, 18*(1), 64–74.

Kittay, E. (1988). Woman as metaphor. *Hypatia, 3*(2), 63–86.

Knox, D. (2019). *The block "all a lie" claim 'bullied' contestants*. https://tvtonight.com.au/2019/10/the-block-all-a-lie-claim-bullied-contestants.html

Knox, D. (2023). *ACMA receives complaints on the block*. https://tvtonight.com.au/2023/10/acma-receives-complaints-on-the-block.html

Legislative Assembly of Queensland. (1997). *Parliamentary Travelsafe Committee Report No. 20* Released pursuant to Section 4(2)(c) of the Parliamentary Papers Act 1995 (May 1997)

Liy, C., Ibrahim, S., Affandi, R., Rosli, N., & Nawi, M. (2017). Causes of fall hazards in construction site management. *International Review of Management and Marketing, 6*(8S), 257–263.

Lowther, A. (2022). *The block's Jenny tells us which NSFW body part she injured in her fall!* https://www.hit.com.au/story/the-block-s-jenny-tells-us-which-nsfw-body-part-she-injured-in-her-fall-209796

Lyall, A. (2020). George and Sarah open up about his big block injury. *The Block.* https://9now.nine.com.au/the-block/2020-george-splinter-infection-medical-centre-joke-story-exclusive/0aab7040-6948-47df-a577-8d8820101e7b www.macmillandictionary.com/dictionary/british/blockhead. Accessed 15 October 2022.

Mantica v Coalroc (No.5) [2022] NSWSC 844.

Mastroianni, B. (2020). *The Block viewers are angry over Keith's comments to a contestant.* https://www.news.com.au/entertainment/tv/reality-tv/the-block-viewers-are-angry-over-keiths-comments-to-a-contestant/news-story/8dbac727d795830496b17f84be9faad6#share-tools. Accessed 17 July 2021.

Meagher, B. R. (2017). Judging the gender of the inanimate: Benevolent sexism and gender stereotypes guide impressions of physical objects. *British Journal of Social Psychology, 56,* 537–560. https://doi.org/10.1111/bjso.12198

Model Managing psychosocial hazards at work Code of Practice (2022). SafeWork Australia.

Muñoz-Laboy, M., Perry, A., Bobet, I., Bobet, S., Ramos, H., Quiñones, F., & Lloyd, K. (2012). The "knucklehead" approach and what matters in terms of health for formerly incarcerated Latino men. *Social Science & Medicine, 74*(11), 1765–1773.

Newman v Andgra Pty Ltd (2002) QGIG 883.

NYCOSH. (2024). *Risks facing women in construction.* https://nycosh.org/wp-content/uploads/2014/09/Women-in-Construction-final-11-8-13-2.pdf

O'Brien, R., Hunt, K., & Hart, G. (2005). It's caveman stuff, but that is to a certain extent how guys still operate: Men's accounts of masculinity and help seeking. *Social Science & Medicine, 61*(3), 503–516. https://doi.org/10.1016/j.socscimed.2004.12.008

Occupational Health and Safety Act 2004 Office of Industrial Relations. (2021). *How to manage work health and safety risks Code of Practice 2021 workplace health and safety Queensland.* AGPS.

Osgood, J., Yates, H., Adler, A., Dyches, K., & Quartana, P. (2021). Tired and angry: Sleep, mental health, and workplace relational aggression. *Military Psychology, 33*(2), 80–91.

Overton, A. R., & Lowry, A. C. (2013). Conflict management: Difficult conversations with difficult people. *Clinics in Colon and Rectal Surgery, 26*(4), 259–264. https://doi.org/10.1055/s-0033-1356728

Paslode. (2020) *Paslode cordless 16 Gauge angled lithium-ion finish Nailer operating manual.* https://www.paslode.com/getmedia/a31d3589-dd6a-4591-9f3a-b7eb21f1e07b/916273-Operator-Manual-for-916200-English.pdf

Pidd, K., Berry, J., Harrison, J., Roche, A., Driscoll, T. R., & Newson, R. (2006). Alcohol and work: Patterns of use, workplace culture and safety. *Injury Research and Statistics Series Number 28* (AIHW cat no. INJCAT 82). AIHW.

Prince v Seven Network (Operations) Limited [2019] NSWWCC 313.

Rinaldi, J., Rice, C., Kotow, C., & Lind, E. (2020). Mapping the circulation of fat hatred. *Fat Studies, 9*(1), 37–50. https://doi.org/10.1080/21604851.2019.1592949

Road Management Act 2004.

Road Safety Act 1986.

Roche, A. M., Bywood, P., Freeman T., Pidd, K., Borlagdan, J., & Trifonoff, A. (2009). *The social context of alcohol use in Australia.* National centre for education and training on addiction.

Roche, A., Chapman, J., Duraisingam, V., Phillips, B., Finnane, J., & Pidd, K. (2020). Construction workers' alcohol use, knowledge, perceptions of risk and workplace norms *Drug Alcohol Review, 39*(7), 941–949.

Rochelle, T. L. (2019). Take a spoonful of concrete and harden the **** up!: How British men in Hong Kong Talk about health and illness. *American Journal of Mens Health, 13*(1), 1557988319829334. https://doi.org/10.1177/1557988319829334

Rosen, N., & Shoenberger, N. (2021). Words speak louder than actions: The connection between gendered language and bullying behavior. *Open Journal of Social Sciences, 9*, 197–214. https://doi.org/10.4236/jss.2021.98014

Safe Work Australia (SWA). (2020). https://covid19.swa.gov.au/covid-19-information-workplaces/industry-information/general-industry-information/hygiene

Safe Work Australia. (2023). *Duties relating to drugs and alcohol.* https://www.safeworkaustralia.gov.au/safety-topic/hazards/drugs-and-alcohol. Accessed 5 May 2023.

SafeWork NSW. (2023). *Slips, trips and falls: On the same level* https://www.safework.nsw.gov.au/hazards-a-z/slips-trips-and-falls-on-the-same-level

Sasangohar, F., Peres, S., Williams, J., Smith, A., & Mannan, M. (2018). Investigating written procedures in process safety: Qualitative data analysis of interviews from high risk facilities. *Process Safety and Environmental Protection, 113*, 30–39.

Savic, M., Room, R., Mugavin, J., Pennay, A., & Livingston, M. (2016). Defining "drinking culture": A critical review of its meaning and connotation in social research on alcohol problems. *Drugs: Education, Prevention and Policy*, 23(4), 270–282. https://doi.org/10.3109/09687637.2016.1153602

Sawicki, M., & Szóstak, M. (2020). Impact of alcohol on occupational health and safety in the construction industry at workplaces with scaffoldings. *Applied Sciences*, 10(19), 6690. https://doi.org/10.3390/app10196690

Shaksepeare. W. (1603). *Shakespeare's Hamlet (A2S2: 192)*. Shakespeare Navigators. http://www.shakespeare-navigators.com/hamlet/H22.html#192

Sleep Health Foundation. (2024). https://www.sleephealthfoundation.org.au/sleep-categories/workplace-health-safety-wellbeing

Spratt, T. (2021). Understanding "fat shaming" in a neoliberal era: Performativity, healthism, and the UK's "obesity epidemic." *Feminist Theory*, 24(1), 86–101.

The Century Dictionary. (1890). (ed. D. Whitey) the Century Co. New York.

Thørrisen, M. M., Skogen, J. C., Bonsaksen, T., Skarpaas, L. S., & Aas, R. W. (2022). Are workplace factors associated with employee alcohol use? The WIRUS cross-sectional study. *BMJ Open*. https://doi.org/10.1136/bmjopen-2022-064352

Vic Roads. (2020). Alcohol and road safety. https://www.vicroads.vic.gov.au/safety-and-road-rules/driver-safety/drugs-and-alcohol/alcohol-and-road-safety#:~:text=This%20is%20an%20offence%20even,passengers%20could%20distract%20a%20driver

WHSQ. (2021). *Managing the risk of falls at workplaces, code of practice*. Queensland Government.

Williamson, A. M., & Feyer, A. (2000). Moderate sleep deprivation produces impairments in cognitive and motor performance equivalent to legally prescribed levels of alcohol intoxication. *Occupational and Environmental Medicine*, 57, 649–655.

Work Health and Safety Act 2011 (Model).

Work Health and Safety Regulation 2011 (Qld).

Worksafe Victoria. (2022). *Planning for safe work-related driving*. https://www.worksafe.vic.gov.au/planning-safe-work-related-driving

CHAPTER 7

Conclusion: Is It Just Me Being a Killjoy and What Are the Public Optics?

Abstract The conclusion in this chapter is that the findings suggest both low order interventions and emerging psychosocial risks at work are socially trivialised in popular cultural settings. Practical applications from this research could result in creating an awareness of these attitudes which in turn may assist agencies to understand how emerging HSW issues are perceived by the viewing audience. Potentially counteracting a dissonance of views about workplace culture and behaviour in popular media could include encouraging workers to accept trivialisation creep may dilute the importance of certain WHSW cognitions. The study creates awareness about contrasting beliefs such as downplaying the tendency to diminish the significance of warning signage, PPE or use of antiquated or insensitive language. People should be encouraged to confront the inconsistency and make positive changes that align with acceptable beliefs and actions. The alternative is to tolerate risk trivialisation but in doing so people risk negative outcomes.

Keywords Audience · Psychosocial hazards · Media concerns · Risk trivialisation

© The Author(s), under exclusive license to Springer Nature Switzerland AG 2024
T. Cvetkovski, *Reality Television and the Art of Trivialising Work Health, Safety and Wellbeing*,
https://doi.org/10.1007/978-3-031-64098-8_7

Reality TV is a core feature of media and cultural studies, but there has not been any research on the impact of reality TV on risk and culture, and how WHSW issues are portrayed in popular culture. This research is timely because it shows how work is performed, or least portrayed through the tele-real lens. This is the first study of its kind to examine a reality TV genre within a health, safety and wellbeing sphere. This research also highlights the fact reality TV contestants on renovation and construction shows are workers conducting work-related activities. Entrenched social beliefs about the level of seriousness of certain tasks suggest dilution of the value of some aspects of HSW in reality TV and risk trivialisation of low order health and safety interventions in popular culture is a mode of cognitive dissonance. Trivialisation as a reductive influence also extends to psychosocial hazards by virtue of specific cultural biases in this reality TV show. To that end, the findings are positively affirmed by the audience and media who have publicly scrutinised events and incidents concerning The Block across several seasons. As authorities responsible for commercial television and advertising standards have recently been notified of socially unacceptable subject matter, such developments reflect a certain shift in peoples' attitudes and beliefs around the portrayal of WHSW in popular culture.

From a sociological perspective, this study has aimed to examine the portrayal of traditional work such as construction and home renovation through the lens of reality TV. It has attempted to demonstrate the importance of popular culture in developing an understanding of WHSW. It has presented a critical analysis of one of the most popular reality TV renovation shows in popular media. The findings from Season 16 of The Block indicate inconsistencies exist in how humans perceive risk because the culture of a workplace is largely shaped by a collective conscience; and the group's solidarity of outlook will determine the organisational risk environment.

If it is accepted the show's influence is broad-spectrum ranging from the housing market to design renovation and construction considerations, then it should be accepted the show is potentially influential in terms of how WHSW is portrayed in construction. It is fair to suggest viewers are entitled to not only enjoy these shows as entertainment, but they are also entitled to responsible portrayal of workplace behaviour. This is because the show offers a behind-the-scenes look at the difficulties, intricacies and pitfalls of home renovation, shedding light on the complexities of construction work. Viewers gain insight into the decision-making process, budgeting considerations, and logistical challenges involved in transforming a space.

The Block demonstrates the complexities and difficulties in the renovation process. It is not only inspirational but also empowering. It is for this reason it bears some responsibility in minimising as much triviality at the worksite as possible. These shows not only provide exposure for industry professionals through marketing and product promotion, but the nature of the work sheds light on exposure to risks and hazards at the construction site that an unskilled worker would fail to appreciate.

It is also accepted study limitations exist such as subjectivity around how many times cables dangled or whether a fleeting image observed was a genuine risk. The author does not cavil with that as satisfactory explanations could readily be provided by the PCBUs around what appeared to be, by way of illustration, questionable placement of gas heaters or lax PPE usage. The rates recorded in the tables and figures may have been lower, but then again, the rates could have been higher as some televised activities may have been missed. The point of the exercise was to determine the quality of the observations and whether they assist in determining organisational maturity from a whole of systems work context. Despite this, the show contained overt elements of conflict, competition and negative interpersonal interactions which appeared concerning at times. When Foreperson Keith commented about Dan's weight in Season 16, the audience was correct to be alarmed. Given the current backlash for Season 19 concerning antisocial activity at this workplace, producers would need to be mindful of the complexities of human experiences, feelings and emotions. To tolerate such conduct can be construed as tacit promotion of exploitation for entertainment.

To that end, the author, however, has not been the first observer to explicate these matters. As set out in the previous chapters, news media and social media continue to take an active interest in unresolved WHSW issues on The Block. While this study is not a media analysis, it would be remiss not to corroborate some of the findings presented in this research with sustained media interest. For example, headlines such as "The Block isn't portraying safety as it should be" (2015), "The Block again under fire over asbestos dust" (2014), or fans remarking on Twitter that "Casual sexism from Scotty, disappointed but not surprised" and "inappropriate jokes about being single" (2018) support the argument that audience does more than watch the show for renovation inspiration or what the judges have to say in room reveals. In New Zealand the following headline garnered national attention "Complaints from viewers could land show 'The Block' in trouble" (2014) and the popular Reality TV podcast *So Dramatic!* Covered *"The Block's "Irresponsible" Conditions Led to Contestants MICROSLEEPING While Driving" (2022)* (emphasis not added). The latter story is particularly relevant here because of the observations made about fatigue, driving as a work-related activity and perceptions about being lazy in Season 16. These newsworthy publications along public commentary via social media raise sustained concerns about contestant welfare, adherence to the media has referred to as "basic health and safety rules" concerning PPE, complex workplace culture and human interactions, and perceptions of risk. Journalists and viewers' comments aside, significant health organisations have also taken interest in WHSW portrayal. The following extract was written by journalist David Knox (2014):

> ***The Block**'s Scott Cam may be an ambassador for Asbestos Awareness Week, but the show is again being criticised by Asbestos Diseases Foundation of Australia.*
>
> *It claims the latest ads for **The Block**: Triple Threat send out a dangerous message.*
>
> *"I was left absolutely speechless, with contestants shown falling through a ceiling, bringing clouds of dust and debris onto unsuspecting home owners, as power tools are shown tearing through the units," the foundation's president Barry Robson says.*
>
> *"This is what happens when TV producers and advertisers, with no understanding of the very real dangers of asbestos, put the promotion of their product above the safety of their viewers."*
>
> <u>*But a Nine spokesperson said there are asbestos warnings on the show's website and a thorough hazardous materials audit is conducted ahead of work beginning*</u> *(emphasis added).*

This extract summarises the risk trivialisation dissonance theory advanced in this research. Just like in the NZ Bisley workwear advertisement justification in Chapter 6 the explanations provided by persons responsible for the work undertaken do not adequately consider the optics of questionable WHSW portrayal. That is, there is nothing entertaining, humorous or positive about falling through voids, penetrations and exposure to nanoparticles. The world has moved beyond silent film Chaplinesque slapstick hazardous physical and psychological comedy.

Unfortunately, these activities perpetuate a poor image of best safety practice. Heightened drama utilised by producers and editors to manipulate situations and promote entertainment value are obvious features of the show. But in the pursuit of high ratings entertainment, producers appear to construct a workplace reality which is incongruent with regulatory expectations. In the absence of consistent compliance, workers' dissonance is encouraged because they are not reminded of cognitions concerned with the importance of HSW.

Irrespective of the creative motivation of the producers, the findings suggest individuals' risk preferences are trivialised as risk management reduction strategies allow for a tolerance in workplace tension and conflict between workers. This mode of dissonance leads to playing down potential hazards and encouraging work around the clock culture. In the show, fatigue and sleep deprivation are not only exploited but lauded as hallmarks of tenacity in a cycle of working around the clock. Hard work is congratulated with reminders about alcohol consumptionwhile still in PPE and onsite. The viewer observes a milieu of work-life imbalance without a sense of what is real or unreal.

The show explicates the reality that cultural biases influence how people interpret, and respond to certain matters at work. It presents to the audience multi-million-dollar construction sites as seen through the lens of ordinary couples competing against each other in a bid to present the best home for auction. Building and then selling homes is a basic human activity. But in the process, this visual experience dilutes or diminishes the value of HSW practice for the price of promoting a distorted workplace reality.

As The Block invites the audience to become emotionally involved in the lives of these ordinary people, it allows the viewers to perhaps feel they can identify with the issues presented. The danger in this, of course, is that with the increase in feelings of identification, there may also be an increase in viewers' perceptions of reality. Viewers may not consider the possibility that subjects may be acting a certain way because producers have encouraged them to act in this way or "play up" certain behaviours. The outcome in any event produces workplace HSW trivialisation.

The literature and case law support the argument that reality TV workplaces are worthy of greater examination because they mirror activities in the workplace. The show depicts scenarios which have not been adequately considered in terms of unacceptable conduct or questionable behaviour at work. As the appetite for renovation shows seem insatiable, it is timely producers of this reality TV genre understand the implications of distorted workplace culture. Understanding cultural factors in risk perception may also assist policy makers and researchers to develop more effective risk communication strategies and interventions that resonate with workers.

The changing nature of appropriate workplace behaviour is complex. Of course The Block was attempting to be as entertaining as commercially possible. But what was so funny about the Greek tradition plate smashing vignette which was a nod to George's Greek heritage in the 21st minute of E46? Was it that George's plate did not smash; or was it because Dave Franklin transformed into Stavros from Athens—replete with a so-called monobrow (unibrow) painted across his forehead along with an upturned moustache? Synophrys relates to eyebrow fusion and is regarded as a variation to "normal" human eyebrow. Kumar (2017: 105) explains, "Besides it is a recognized feature of Cornelia De Lange syndrome and many other genetic disorders associated with it". Of course, the response to the above question by the producers would be it was performed in jest and that no harm was intended. The same justifications would no doubt be applied to use of phrases like Knucklehead and "You will be on the market now. Or off the market…A couple of good sorts with plenty of cash" (Cam Scott in Halfpenny, 2018). This news story by Bervanakis (2018) was entitled "The Block's Scott Cam angers viewers who label him 'sexist'"; and because the affable host has a "laid-back larrikin attitude", the comments are transformed in something innocuous. Is this benevolent sexism? The viewer is entitled to query whether these representations mean the show has now provided financial security for two young women; and when combined with favourable physical attributes, potential partners will now find them worthy.

It was not the point of this undertaking to investigate humour and social interaction at work, but the nature of the humour on the show does highlight the trivial consideration of the importance of how words and gestures are perceived in the public sphere. Of course comedians and artists have relied on WHS content in their repertoires. For example, Australian comedian Steve Hughes (2021) performs very funny health and safety comedy routines about OHS over-regulation. Punk-rant duo Sleaford Mods have satirised UK OHS inspectors, venue compliance and health and safety generally.[1] Popular Australian comedian Merrick Watts has performed a ridiculous sketch poking fun at workplace signage, PPE, and falls from heights in *Thank God you're here safety officers*. YouTube is replete with making light of WHSW activities. But that is entertainment in the form of satire. The context of The Block and renovation reality TV generally are not premised on comedy.

The appeal of The Block reminds the audience that unreserved dedication to a work project leads to lucrative reward. This might explain the desire for people to project in the public sphere otherwise routine tasks such as renovating homes as they strive to self-actualise or self-realise their own potential as builders and renovators. In the spectacle, however, the findings demonstrate trivialising WHSW for the purposes of satisfying audience desire to consume popular culture. Cultural Risk Theory provides a nuanced framework for understanding the complex interplay between culture, risk perception, and societal dynamics. By acknowledging the cultural dimensions of risk, policy makers, practitioners, and researchers can develop more contextually relevant and effective strategies for managing risks, enhancing resilience, and promoting societal wellbeing.

The Block is produced for entertainment and commercialisation purposes, but the work undertaken is serious. The best evidence for that proposition is the fact the completed homes are sold for several million dollars. The other indicator The Block is a serious show is the fact complaints or concerns have been voiced by viewers through social media, traditional media and to authorities. The audience does voice its dissent when questionable workplace activities occur during the undertaking. This research is empirically validated because audiences do seem to care about what is depicted. As such this research is far from being based on abstract conceptions of cultural theory of risk and trivialisation dissonance. Reality TV provides an opportunity for greater of workplace cultural exchanges and it is hoped insights can be gained in terms of how WHSW is depicted through a popular cultural lens.

---

[1] See for example in a live recording in C. Franz (2017). "Bunch of Kunst," DVD Book, Harbinger Sound.

REFERENCES

Bervanakis, M. (2018). *The Block's Scott Cam angers viewers who label him 'sexist'*. https://www.news.com.au/entertainment/tv/reality-tv/the-blocks-scott-cam-angers-viewers-who-label-him-sexist/news-story/8af605f100e1137841749fe0311cb76f

Halfpenny, K. (2018). Bianca and Carla say they're down with Scott Cam's 'sexist' comment on *The Block*. *The New Daily*. https://www.thenewdaily.com.au/entertainment/tv/2018/10/29/scott-cam-sexist-the-block

Hughes, S. (2021). *Health and safety & offended comedy routines YouTube*. https://www.youtube.com/watch?v=vbsHox73mRo

Knox, D. (2014). *The Block again under fire over asbestos dust*. https://tvtonight.com.au/2014/12/the-block-again-under-fire-over-asbestos-dust.html

Kumar, P. (2017). Synophrys: Epidemiological study. *International of Journal Trichology*, 9(3), 105–107. https://doi.org/10.4103/ijt.ijt_14_17

NZ Herald. (2016). *Complaints from viewers could land show 'The Block' in trouble*. https://www.nzherald.co.nz/entertainment/complaints-from-viewers-could-land-show-the-block-in-trouble/7BCC2TUEIMXHTCBXJSNLDHLJBU/

Safety Nerd. (2015). *The Block isn't portraying safety as it should be*. https://safetyrisk.net/the-block-isnt-portraying-safety-as-it-should-be/

So Dramatic! (2022). *The Block's "irresponsible" conditions led to contestants microsleeping while driving*. https://sodramaticonline.com/2022/10/25/the-block-driving-conditions-microsleeping/

Sleaford Mods. (2017). In C. Franz. introduction to "Routine Dean" live in *Bunch of Kunst*, DVD Book, Harbinger Sound.

Watts, M. (2010). *Thank god you're here safety officers YouTube*. https://www.youtube.com/watch?v=hybEUXwVZHQ

Index

A
administrative control, 10, 45, 79
aggression, 4, 20, 54, 72, 103, 112, 117, 121, 136
alcohol consumption, 12, 20, 103, 105–107, 122, 126, 129, 138, 140, 155
alcohol normalisation, 103, 108
alcohol tolerance, 105
anti-discrimination, 112
asbestos, 6–8, 44, 89, 153, 154
audience, 5–7, 13, 21, 22, 26, 28, 32, 33, 36, 37, 39, 40, 64, 68, 73, 152, 153, 155, 157
Australian Communications and Media Authority (ACMA), 24–26, 84, 123

B
best practices, 3, 15, 24, 79, 84, 113
Bisley Workwear, 15, 37, 72, 73
Bisley Workwear advertisement, 154

The Block, 7, 9, 15, 22, 26, 27, 32, 37, 39, 40, 44, 47, 71, 84, 111, 122, 152, 157
The Block contestants, 2, 5, 9
body image, 118–120
Body of Knowledge, 64
building site, 71–73, 108
building work, 2
bullying, 4, 20–22, 26, 84, 103, 112, 118, 119, 123

C
Cam, Scott, 7, 68, 72, 99, 113, 138, 154
Carlsberg beer commercial, 108
causation, 113
Channel 9, 7, 26
clutter, 3, 46, 52, 80, 81, 85–102, 132. *See also* mess
Code of Practice (CoP), 4, 24, 81, 103, 112
coding, 52, 53, 56, 60

cognitive bias, 45, 47
cognitive dissonance, 10, 13, 55, 152
collective conscience, 10, 46, 106, 152
competition, 33, 153
conflict, 4, 5, 12, 32, 112, 142, 155
confusion, 27
construction work, 5, 6, 27, 65, 75, 121, 152
content analysis, 53–55, 60
Covid 19, 14, 26–28, 35, 79, 84, 94, 117
co-workers, 73, 103, 108
cultural bias, 5, 9, 12, 44–46, 48, 54, 55, 76, 152, 155
Cultural Risk Theory/Cultural Theory of risk (CRT/CTR), 9, 11, 44, 46, 52, 157
Cultural Theory (CT), 9, 55

D
danger, 38, 44, 155
dangling cords, 15, 80, 98
data, 5, 11, 12, 44, 53, 55, 61, 79, 106
discrimination policies, 112
dissonance, 3, 5, 10, 13, 46, 47, 78, 155
disturbance, 121
Do-it-Yourself (DIY), 37, 55, 63
Douglas. M., 5, 9, 44, 48
downplaying, 5, 10, 13, 47
driving, 78, 99, 135, 154
dust, 7, 62, 89, 98, 101, 154

E
electrical work, 13, 66
environment, 2, 4, 15, 21, 32, 45, 56, 71, 74, 79, 98, 105, 112, 117, 152
essential work, 27

exploitative practices, 32
exposure, 11, 15, 21, 22, 25, 52, 65, 71, 72, 76, 78, 153, 154

F
falls from height, 65, 157
fatigue, 4, 40, 81, 103, 112, 121, 137, 154, 155
fatshaming, 22, 118–120
food, 12, 37, 38, 80, 83, 84, 99, 120

G
gender, 71, 103, 109, 111
gestures, 26, 109, 111, 112, 140, 156
goggles, 73, 74
good work design, 15
gratuitous comments, 109, 111

H
harassment, 22, 26, 112, 115, 116, 119, 123
harden up, 68, 71–74
hard hats, 33, 75, 76, 86, 87, 89, 95
harm, 2–4, 22–25, 32, 44–46, 71, 72, 76, 77, 79–81, 103, 105, 112
hazard, 4, 5, 10–12, 22, 25, 45–47, 52, 64, 77, 79, 80, 105, 111, 112, 115, 118, 139, 152, 155
hierarchy of needs, 36, 37
High Visibility (Hi-Viz), 12–14, 78, 90, 108, 124, 129
home renovation, 35, 152
horseplay. *See* skylarking
House Rules, 20, 112
hygiene, 11, 12, 52, 70, 80, 83–102, 122

I
injuries, 11, 21, 45, 63–66, 69–71, 76, 80, 81, 83, 95

intangible, 2, 4, 52, 56, 60, 103, 104
interpersonal, 121, 153
interpersonal conflict, 112, 115
interventions, 12, 13, 68, 70, 103, 152, 156
ISO Standard 6385, 15

J
Jetfire, 56, 68, 91, 98, 99
Jetfire gas heater, 68

K
knucklehead, 110, 111, 137, 156

L
language, 10, 11, 20, 52, 109–111, 114, 115, 124–144
lax PPE, 11, 52, 61, 68, 78, 85–102, 153
lazy, 120–121, 123, 125, 131, 139, 154
legislation, 20, 21, 23, 25, 71, 107
Loose cables, 15, 82
low-order controls, 76, 78
LPG, 56, 67, 86, 91, 94, 99

M
Makita, 15, 96
male dominated, 70, 71, 109, 110
manning it out, 71, 72
masks, 6, 27, 79, 87, 89, 90, 95, 103
Maslow, Abraham, 37
McDonalds, 37, 99
measurement, 10, 55
medical attention, 69–71, 127
mental state, 118, 119
mess, 40, 52, 80, 82, 83, 97, 98, 124
method, 55, 62
mixed methods, 53–55

My Kitchen Rules (MKR), 20, 22

N
nail gun, 62, 75, 77, 85, 93, 95, 101
Network Seven, 20
9 (Nine) Now, 38

O
observational approach, 11, 52
Obsessive Compulsive Disorder (OCD), 4, 124, 142
Occupational Health and Safety (OHS), 23, 78
onsite, 7, 11, 27, 46, 52, 61, 82, 83, 90, 108, 117, 126, 155

P
paint, 91, 99, 113
Paslode, 62
perception, 11, 12, 44, 52, 73, 83, 116
Personal Protective Equipment (PPE), 3, 7, 14, 35, 47, 71, 75, 78, 89, 93, 99, 155
Person Conducting a Business or Undertaking (PCBU), 23
physical state, 118, 119
power tools, 63, 82, 93, 98, 105, 124, 154
Prince decision, 23
prize money, 36, 112
protection of worker, 23
psychological injury, 4, 20–22
psychosocial, 2, 4, 11, 13, 20, 22, 26, 44, 47, 52, 56, 60, 84, 103, 111, 112, 115, 120, 123, 139, 152
psychosocial codes, 40
public scrutiny, 108

Q
questionable workplace behaviour, 60

R
Reality TV (Television), 2, 5, 7, 9, 11, 14, 15, 20, 22–25, 27, 31, 32, 35, 37, 39, 44, 71, 122, 152, 155, 157
reductionist thinking, 68
regulations, 3, 22, 24, 26
regulator, 22, 66, 86, 103
Reilly, Dan, 35
renovation, 2, 6, 7, 20, 124, 152, 153, 155
risk, 3, 4, 10, 13, 44–48, 61, 62, 64, 65, 72, 152, 156
Risk Analysis (RA), 9
Risk and Culture, 9, 44, 152
risk perception, 9, 10, 44–46, 55, 157
risk-taking, 10, 45, 47
risk trivialisation, 3, 5, 13, 46, 47, 54, 68, 152

S
Safe Work Australia (SWA), 65, 106
Schleiger, Keith, 35
signage, 3, 10–13, 45, 52, 71, 75, 76, 79, 85, 95, 157
skylarking, 11, 52, 61, 63, 78, 95, 97, 101
slip trip fall, 88
social media, 5, 20–22, 39, 153, 157
societal dynamics, 157
solidarities of outlook, 48
splinter injury, 68
Stakeholders, 25
status quo, 47, 114, 115
stereotypes, 70, 109–112
stress, 4, 13, 40, 46, 123, 125, 141
syllogism, 64, 65
system of work, 2, 14, 56, 80, 81, 83, 85, 124

T
tangible, 6, 11, 32, 60, 61, 80, 103
tension, 4, 112, 121, 126, 129, 130, 134, 142, 155
theoretical underpinnings, 9, 10
tools, 35, 62, 80, 88, 92, 96, 101, 107
toxic workplace, 113, 116
tradespeople (tradies), 8, 13, 72, 140
trivialisation, 3, 10, 13, 15, 48, 60, 74, 111
trivialisation dissonance, 3, 10, 11, 15, 46, 63, 70, 154, 157
TV codes of practice, 24

U
unacceptable workplace practices, 15
unsecured loads, 77
untidiness, 5, 11, 52. *See also* clutter; mess

V
villain, 20, 21, 131

W
Wildavsky, A., 5, 9, 44, 48
wolf whistle, 111, 125, 135, 143
work at height, 44, 45, 65
work ethic, 11
Work Health and Safety Act (WHS Act), 23, 72
working at height, 3, 45, 65
workplace culture, 3, 12, 13, 20, 21, 26, 70, 103, 106, 108, 112, 154, 156

Workplace health, safety and wellbeing
(WHSW/HSW), 2, 3, 5, 10, 13,
15, 45, 52, 55, 76, 105, 122,
152, 154, 155, 157

workplace policy, 105, 106
worksite, 12, 23, 35, 69, 71, 72, 80,
85, 94, 105, 108, 110, 120, 129,
132, 140, 153